THE
QUEEN'S
ENGLISH
AND HOW TO USE IT

THE QUEEN'S ENGLISH

AND HOW TO USE IT

BERNARD C. LAMB

PRESIDENT OF THE QUEEN'S ENGLISH SOCIETY

Michael O'Mara Books Limited

This paperback edition first published in 2015

First published in Great Britain in 2010 by
Michael O'Mara Books Limited
9 Lion Yard
Tremadoc Road
London SW4 7NQ

A CIP catalogue record for this book is available from the British Library.

Papers used by Michael O'Mara Books Limited are natural, recyclable
products made from wood grown in sustainable forests. The manufacturing
processes conform to the environmental regulations of the country of origin.

ISBN: 978-1-78243-434-4 in paperback print format
ISBN: 978-1-84317-482-0 in hardback print format
ISBN: 978-1-84317-753-1 in EPub format
ISBN: 978-1-84317-754-8 in Mobipocket format

2 3 4 5 6 7 8 9 10

Illustrations by Andrew Pinder

Cover design by James Empringham

Designed and typeset by K.DESIGN, Winscombe, Somerset

Printed and bound by CPI Group (UK) Ltd, Croydon, CR0 4YY

www.mombooks.com

Contents

Acknowledgements

At Michael O'Mara Books, I am very grateful to Michael O'Mara for suggesting this book, to Toby Buchan for his encouragement, and to Anna Marx for her perceptive editing.

The chapter on business writing was very kindly provided by Sidney Callis, business writer.

Members of the Queen's English Society I wish to thank include Martin Estinel, Bill Ball and Ken Thomson for their many valuable comments, and Ray Ward, Michael Gorman, Mike Plumbe, Brenda Lamb, Rhea Williams, John Lamb, Malcolm Skeggs, Pat Brown, Anne Shelley and Prue Raper for their helpful contributions. Any remaining errors are the author's responsibility.

My parents, Ernest and Jacqueline Lamb, gave me many useful lessons in life, including a love of reading. A writing group started in Richmond by Joan Murray Simpson taught me to accept constructive criticism and gave me extensive practice in writing and meeting deadlines. Dr Rupa Wickramaratne improved my spelling and my Scrabble.

CHAPTER 1

Introduction

The aims of this book

This is a direct, practical book to help people to use the best and most influential form of English, **the Queen's English**. That means to write and speak clear, correct, conventional British English. The Queen's English is not some high-flown exclusive form but is the most widely used standard version. It is much valued by employers, who want their employees to be literate and to give a good impression of their firm

We use English for five prime purposes: reading, writing, speaking, listening and almost constantly for thinking. The better our English is, the better we can do these things. There are thoughts that we cannot consciously have unless we have the right words and an ability to use them in coherent sentences.

English consists of the words, which are the **vocabulary** or lexicon, and **grammar**, which is how the words fit together to make sense.

It is best to read this book from beginning to end but there is no harm in looking at any section of particular relevance to you whenever you wish. There is a small amount of repetition between chapters to make each more self-contained. Repetition is a great way to learn.

This book cannot cover all points. Further information can be found in works in the Bibliography, pages 240–2.

Why having good English is essential

Good English is needed for work and leisure. The heads of firms such as Marks & Spencer, BT and Tesco, of organisations such as the Confederation of British Industry and the Institute of Directors, and of many commercial firms, universities and other educational establishments, have complained recently of the poor standards of English of many of their job applicants and employees.

The head of an online recruitment agency wrote that one third of job applications from graduates with good degrees from good universities were immediately turned down because of poor English in their CVs and covering letters. Their errors showed poor attention to detail, ignorance and a bad attitude.

If people make bad mistakes in their grammar, spelling or punctuation, what faith can you have in their reliability? Could you trust their calculations in finance or engineering, such as cost estimates or building plans? Would you want to employ them, and have them give a bad impression of your firm?

This book describes the most common errors made, and how to identify, correct and avoid them. Explanations are given as to why particular usages are right or wrong, or acceptable or unacceptable. Practice is given in spotting errors and rectifying them.

Different attitudes to English are illustrated in my double limerick:

FOOLISH AND WISE LITERATURE TEACHERS

> *A professor once told his tutees:*
> > *'Write English just as you please.*
> > *Grammatical rules*
> > *Are simply for fools,*
> > *And spelling is only for bees.'*
>
> *His colleague said: 'No. To excel*
> *You've got to use English so well;*
> *If you know how it works*
> *You can cope with its quirks*
> *And write books which can easily sell.'*

Expanding your vocabulary

It really pays to build up your vocabulary for understanding the words which others use, and for your own use. It is embarrassing when someone uses a word which you do not know and need to grasp. The better your **knowledge of words**, the richer, more complete and precise will be your use and understanding of speech and writing. You are strongly advised to look up in a dictionary any words you are unsure of, in this book or elsewhere.

It can be a matter of life or death to have the correct understanding of **health advice and medical reports**, but words used in medicine can be difficult for the layman even though they are often built with common prefixes and suffixes. There is a special emphasis on such understanding here.

There are situations in English where **opinions differ** or **acceptable alternatives** exist, as in the spelling of *aging/ageing*, *burnt/burned*, *authorised/authorized*, or *stadiums/stadia*. Even eminent grammarians often disagree over whole systems of grammar and word classification.

The attitude here is that it does not matter whether the word *whose* is called a determiner or a possessive adjective. What is important is that *whose* is the possessive form of *who* and must never be confused with *who's*, a contraction of *who is* or *who has*.

It has been said that 'A *word means whatever I want it to mean*,' but if people use the same word with different meanings, misunderstandings arise, sometimes serious. If a child says, 'My *stepfather is really wicked*,' does that mean that the stepfather is awful or wonderful? One cannot tell. The need for **mutual understanding** is paramount.

The value of knowing common rules of English

Learning the **common rules** of English can be very rewarding. It helps to have explained the reasons for what you may have been doing already; it can resolve doubts and uncertainties, and lead to correction of errors. Rules are needed for a language but some may be broken for special effect, such as surprise, humour or dramatic effect. The better you understand the rules, the better you can use special effects, for example in jokes, social letters, poetry or drama.

Here are three cases where knowing the rules really helps.
The rules will be explained in the appropriate chapters. (i),
When do you use singular or plural verbs with collective
nouns: *The committee has*, or *The committee have*? (ii), When
do you use *I* or *me*, in *John and I*, or *John and me*? (iii), Why
does *Worm was slow* sound wrong, while *The worm was slow*
and *Worms are slow* sound right?

Understanding grammatical rules and terms

To understand the rules, it is necessary to learn some of the words
used in discussing grammar. Much of grammar is not taught in
schools in Britain today, or is taught badly and unenthusiastically.
Even those who were taught grammar at school have often
forgotten most of it, so the **basic facts** are given here about verbs,
nouns, adjectives, adverbs, prepositions, etc., to enable everyone
to get those things right.

In this book, the necessary words are introduced gradually,
in context, with a glossary towards the end as an easy-reference
back-up. Many words will be familiar already, such as *noun*,
subject, *adjective* and *tense*. They will be introduced in **bold
type**, while examples will be in *italics*. **Definitions**, **rules** and
keywords when first introduced will be given in **bold type**. Some
grammatical terms look like ordinary words but have specific
meanings, such as *simple sentence* and *complex sentence*.

The **aspects of grammar** covered are those with the most
practical applications, such as subject/verb agreement, getting

the tenses right, how to form plurals correctly, how to detect and remedy incomplete sentences, and how to connect sentences.

Here is an example of how **simple knowledge** can resolve a word confusion. Suppose you were unsure of whether to write *He was formally elected chairman* or *He was formerly elected chairman*. Either could be correct. Knowing that adverbs are usually formed by adding *-ly* to the adjective, we can see that the first sentence refers to a *formal* election, one following established procedure, while the second refers to a *former* election, a previous one. The problem is thus easily solved from basic knowledge about adjectives and adverbs.

A word's **grammatical function** can affect its meaning and pronunciation. Consider the meanings of the verb *to prune* and the noun, *a prune*. *To entrance*, as by magic, has the stress on the long second syllable, *-ance*, while *the entrance* has the stress on the first syllable and a short *-ance* sound.

Using punctuation for clear, easily understood English

The chapter on punctuation (pages 96–121) includes clear guidance on using apostrophes, commas, semicolons and colons. If you master those, your punctuation will be far above average. All the punctuation marks and other typographical devices, such as **bold type** and *italics*, are covered.

Spelling matters

Your spelling can give a good impression or a bad one. The advice on **spelling** includes **useful rules** and **ways of remembering** tricky spellings. Learning about **prefixes**, **suffixes** and **word origins** greatly helps with spelling and meaning. By looking at prefixes and suffixes in the chapter on spelling, pages 153–66, you can work out that *gastritis* is an inflammation of the stomach and that *pyromania* is a compulsion to set things on fire, even if you have never met those words before.

Even if you think that you are a bad speller by nature, you can still remedy that weakness, as I managed to in my thirties. A foreign research student pointed out politely that my work was full of spelling errors. This was humiliating but very useful. I began to use a dictionary much more and to learn rules of spelling, while learning about word origins proved interesting and helpful.

Getting the sentences right

Using grammar and punctuation to get the sentences right is really fundamental, and most errors are easy to identify and remedy.

Sir Winston Churchill wrote of his schooldays at Harrow:

> By being so long in the lowest form I gained an immense advantage over the cleverer boys . . . I got into my bones the essential structure of the normal British sentence – which is a noble thing.

Style and writing well

To write well, you need to be in command of the word, the sentence, the paragraph and the structure of the whole piece. Getting a coherent, logical **flow of information** or ideas is really important. Choices of words, sentence structure and paragraphing all affect style. You need to follow the established conventions of formal writing but do not need any exam passes or other academic qualifications in English to write well – just knowledge and care.

It is wrong to use specialist terms for a general readership. For example, a report on the AXA Framlington European Fund contained this sentence: *We are primarily a bottom-up, active equity manager*. The term *bottom-up* is not explained and is presumably jargon. Are they face-down?

Testing helps you to learn

There are self-test sections, usually with the answers given. Do try these short exercises (about ten to twenty minutes each), for example, **error-spotting**, as they will engage your brain and strongly reinforce information given in the main text. The **vocabulary challenge** asks you to check whether you know precisely what each word means, or asks you to distinguish the difference in meaning between two or more words.

Through trying the tests and reading the answers, you can develop your knowledge of English and expand your vocabulary. Try some of the exercises with your friends as they are good fun. The error-spotting tests often evoke peals of laughter at the worst mistakes.

Examples of excellent English

In contrast to the many illustrations of poor English, there are examples of excellent modern English, written in different styles. While you will have your own style or styles of writing, it is worth seeing how others have achieved particular effects in theirs. There are many kinds of writing which you might wish to use at different times: direct and plain; rich and lyrical; humorous; persuasive; affectionate; apologetic; short or extended; formal or informal; general or technical; fiction or non-fiction. All can be achieved by using good Queen's English.

CHAPTER 2

What is the Queen's English and why should one use it?

🌺 The Queen's English

The Queen's English means straightforward standard British English. It is the most authoritative and easily understood form of the language throughout the world, used in non-fiction, fiction and poetry. Textbooks use it, as do newspapers, businesses, government documents, air-traffic controllers, and ordinary people in private and work correspondence. It can be used well or badly. This book deals mainly with **written English** but also gives guidance on **spoken English**.

The Queen's English can be spoken in a variety of **accents**. It does not have to be spoken in what has been called 'received pronunciation', 'Oxford English' or 'BBC English'. It is useful, practical English, not exclusive or elitist. A spoken version called 'the Queen's English' is widely preferred for its clarity to any other form.

The term 'the Queen's English' dates back to 1592, in the time of Queen Elizabeth I, but using the Queen's English is not the prerogative of royalty or any class, group, region or country. The *Oxford English Dictionary* defines it as: *'the English language as regarded as under the guardianship of the Queen; hence, standard or correct English'*. This book is a guide to using it well and purposefully; it is a practical manual, not a complicated treatise on linguistics.

The **first recorded printed reference** to the Queen's English, as listed in the *Oxford English Dictionary*, is *He must be running on the letter, and abusing the Queenes English without pittie or mercie.* (1592, T. Nashe, *Strange Newes.*) Another early reference to the monarch's English also involves abusing it. In Shakespeare's *The Merry Wives of Windsor*, Act 1, Scene IV, Mistress Quickly says,

> *What: John Rugby! – I pray thee, go to the casement, and see if you can see my master, Doctor Caius, coming; if he do, i'faith, and find any body in the house, here will be an old abusing of God's patience, and the king's English.*

In spite of today's long and expensive education in schools, there is still far too much abusing of the Queen's English.

The phrase **'The King's English'** was used by Thomas Wilson in *Arte of Rhetorique* in 1553, where he deplored departures from plain speech and the infection of English with fancy foreign borrowings. The separation of 'King's English' or 'Queen's English' from association with particular monarchs is demonstrated by the case of King George I (1660–1727) who came from Hanover and spoke very little English.

The word **'English'** was applied to the language before it was used for the people, and occurs in writings from about AD 880.

By the early fifteenth century, 'court English', as opposed to 'country English', was partly standardised for government use. When William Caxton set up his printing business in Westminster in 1476, his choice of what to publish helped to standardise English.

The society which promotes the better use and understanding of the Queen's English is **The Queen's English Society** (pages 243–8). Its website is www.queens-english-society.org, which contains a lot of helpful advice and information.

Why and when one should use the Queen's English

English is a subtle yet powerful language, capable of delicate nuances of meaning, as well as expressing ideas simply and directly. Good users of **standard English** have the advantages of accuracy and clarity, aiding their powers of conveying facts, ideas and emotions to others, and of being unambiguous, correct and persuasive. Because it is standard, many people automatically use the Queen's English without being conscious of doing so; that does not mean that their usage is free of common errors.

The **standard form of a language** is the one which all its users should be able to understand, wherever they come from. They should be able to use it for general communication, although they may prefer a local form for **local communication**.

There are many **variants of British English**, including regional and ethnic versions in Britain, as well as foreign 'Englishes' such as Indian or American English.

Foreigners often use something approaching standard English to communicate with each other if they do not speak each other's language or dialect. In England one frequently hears students from Hong Kong speaking English with students from other parts of China, because spoken Cantonese is so different from Mandarin Chinese, although they largely share the same written language.

The Queen's English, with correct grammar and vocabulary, can be spoken in many accents, including foreign ones, say Indian or Canadian, and regional British accents, such as those used in Birmingham, Newcastle or Glasgow. There are extremely good users of the Queen's English in Sri Lanka and India, and some very bad users among native speakers in London, Cambridge and Oxford. There is ignorance, carelessness and deliberate 'dumbing down'. In **spoken English**, we often use **incomplete sentences** which would be wrong in written English, such as, *'Got enough cake?'*, *'Want a cuppa?'* or *'Going out now'*.

Standard English should be used when writing business letters, essays, reports, job applications and on all formal occasions. Most people use it automatically nearly all the time. Other forms of English are completely acceptable in appropriate situations. For example, in a play involving characters with **strong regional** or **ethnic dialects**, the author would not write standard English for their speech. Their different usages of English would be part of their characterisation. In radio plays, it is common to have different characters of the same sex talking with different accents to help listeners determine who is speaking.

Non-standard English includes shortened forms used in text messaging, such as *c u l8er* for *See you later*. The lively poetry of Robert Burns contains too many Scottish or dialect words, and too many non-English spellings, to be standard English, e.g., *gaed*, *waefu'*, *walie*, *nieve* and *thrissle*. A problem with non-standard usages is that they can cause confusion. Examples from Malaysia include *to have an off-day*, meaning *to have a day off*, not a bad day, and *to chop a document*, meaning to rubber-stamp it, not to cut it. There is much bad English produced in Britain from ignorance, carelessness and a fear of seeming 'posh'.

Here are **four examples** which do not fit the Queen's English:

'*When I missed that penalty, I was literally gutted.*' The footballer was disappointed but had not had his innards removed, unlike criminals hundreds of years ago who were hanged, drawn and quartered. He misused the word *literally*;

'I was literally gutted.'

if something literally happens, it really does happen. *To be gutted* is something which literally happens to fish and edible animals, but has become a fashionable metaphor to mean disappointed.

'You don't know nuffin'.' This is the use of a double negative with the sense of a single negative: *You do not know anything.* It is illogical, as someone who does not know nothing must know something. *'Nuffin'* or *'nuffink'* is a bad pronunciation of *'nothing'*.

''Tis ternite, innit?' Using *'Tis* for *It is* is acceptable in speech but is not usual in written prose. *Ternite* is a bad pronunciation of *tonight*, and *innit?* is a slovenly way of saying *isn't it?*

Overheard on a train: *'Me and him gets on great.'* This should be: *'He and I get on well.'* The two pronouns should be in the subject case, not the object case; the verb should be plural as there are two subjects, and *great* is an adjective when an adverb is needed. One should list oneself last.

I use **'low English'** to describe such bad English. It is ungrammatical, badly pronounced and poorly enunciated, with a severely restricted vocabulary, and usually laden with swear words. It suggests that its users are coarse, uneducated and unintelligent.

One also gets **corrupted English** for reasons other than ignorance, especially in advertising. There may be different spellings, such as *lite* and *nite*, perhaps to catch the eye for being non-standard. The corruption may involve slogans such as *Beanz Meanz Heinz*, *Drinka pinta milka day*, or expressions such as *Pick 'n'mix*. Do not use such English yourself.

Headlines are a source of poor English, especially when punctuation is missing. One might see a headline such as:

IS NO 10 HIDING THE DIRT
asks Jeremy Lane

There should be a question mark after the question and the headline only makes sense if readers interpret *NO* as *No.*, meaning *number*, and *NO 10* as *10 Downing Street*, meaning the government.

Even nationally important firms produce poor or wrong English. A Waitrose label was an awful jumble of unpunctuated words:

BRITISH FREE RANGE DRY CURED MOLASSES
ROAST HAMPSHIRE GAMMON HAM

There are a number of ambiguities there. If the compound adjective *free-range* is not hyphenated, could the shopper claim that the product was free of charge?

TESCO 4 WHITE HOT CROSS BUNS

Are those buns white or white-hot; are they cross? All users of English should know about hyphens and compound adjectives (pages 109–11).

There are some cases where non-standard English is permissible. In **obituaries**, the subject of sentences may often be omitted when it is the name of the person who died – after that has been firmly established – to avoid excessive repetition of that name, e.g., *Postwar, ran the Geography Department at St Edwards School in Oxford and became master of Field House*. Similarly, in a **CV** which is clearly about oneself one might use an incomplete sentence such as *Went to Imperial College, 1998–2001*.

Learning to improve one's English

Native speakers learn English by being taught by parents, other relatives, teachers and friends, initially by hearing others speak, and later by contact with the written word and from hearing broadcasts. Very young children typically make many errors, especially in grammar, but learn by being repeatedly corrected. Some grammatical rules are largely mastered by experience, but in children of an appropriate age they can be learnt more certainly by being taught explicitly. Many adults do not know the rules of grammar which they use every day. Knowing the rules makes for better, more confident usage.

Punctuation and spelling are best taught explicitly and by correction, as picking them up by reading is haphazard. Reading examples of good English is excellent practice but is not enough to teach children or adults how to write correctly and expressively themselves. It is extremely helpful to have explicit rules, so this book gives explicit rules for grammar, punctuation, spelling and word choice. Many words are frequently confused, conveying quite the wrong meaning, such as *affect/effect* and *complimentary/ complementary*.

Punctuation is absolutely necessary to convey the correct meaning in the most easily understood way. The correct punctuation is that which makes the meaning clearest. Even if one's grammar and punctuation are correct, it is still essential to select the right word for the intended meaning, and to have a large general **vocabulary**. A **speciality-specific vocabulary** may also be needed.

Grammar, the rules about how words fit together to give meaning, is essential. It can be taught through rules, background knowledge and examples.

In writing, one can be absolutely **clear** or be deliberately **obscure** (as in many political speeches and commercial negotiations), but **ambiguity** should be intentional, not from carelessness or ignorance.

✑ The practical use of the Queen's English in speech

'The Queen's English' usually refers to the written form of standard British English, but has also been used of a spoken version known as 'received pronunciation', 'Oxford English' or 'BBC English'. The BBC employs many people whose spoken English is poor in grammar and clarity, sometimes with impenetrably strong regional accents which listeners from other areas find hard to understand. Fortunately, one can still routinely hear **excellent clear spoken English** from the newsreaders in the morning on BBC Radio 3.

In 2006, **CoPilot Live mobile phone satellite navigation** published the results of their survey of people in different parts of Britain as to **what form of spoken English they wanted** for the voice of their **satellite navigation** device. The press release concluded that:

> *Speaking elegantly and with proper prose is no longer reserved for royalty and grammatical sticklers; it's the language we want our gadgets speaking too . . . The **Queen's English** was judged by far the most popular voice for Sat-Nav, with more than half of people (57%) saying that they wouldn't take orders from any other regional accent.*

> *. . . The crisp, clear tones of Queen's English are favoured significantly over other regional dialects. People from every single region in Britain voted the accent their favourite – even in Northern Ireland, Scotland and Wales.*

The runner-up accent was Irish – Dublin, with 19 per cent of the votes.

The report quoted me as 'Spokesperson for the Queen's English Society':

> *For something as important as getting your directions right then clarity is paramount. What matters most is a form of English that is most understandable by the majority. It's clearest in pronunciation and clearest in grammatical structure. In other words it doesn't have the idiosyncrasies that some local accents and dialects have. Queen's English is by far the most widely understood form of English in the UK.*

My view is that **regional accents** can be enjoyable and should not be denigrated. They can help to give a local sense of identity, but for understandability at national and international levels, standard Queen's English is best. One would not want pilots on foreign planes misunderstanding landing instructions when given in some unfamiliar regional accent or dialect. For spoken English, see pages 224–9.

CHAPTER 3

The main ways to improve one's English

There are two main ways to improve one's English: learning to spot, correct and **avoid errors**, and **improving one's style**.

To write good standard English, **the Queen's English**, one needs the following, which are covered in other chapters:

- careful checking for sense, accuracy and conciseness
- correct grammar, spelling, punctuation and word choice
- a large vocabulary
- the appropriate style
- a logical flow of information or ideas.

Dictionaries. For spelling, word choice, meaning and pronunciation, you are strongly advised to use a **comprehensive dictionary** which gives the **pronunciation** and **origin** of each word. It is worth looking at the dictionary's instructions to see how it works. See how it represents the sounds of words and where the stresses fall. For example, *invalid* as a noun has the stress on the first syllable, but the adjective *invalid* (not valid), is stressed on the second syllable.

When looking up a word in a dictionary, beware of silent letters as in *knack, write, psychopath, gnat* and *llama.* There are electronic dictionaries and crossword-solvers which suggest 'sound-alike' words with different spellings.

Correct word choice means not confusing similar words of different meaning, such as *affect* and *effect*: see pages 167–75. To find words of similar meaning, you can use a **thesaurus**, such as *Roget's*, or a **synonym dictionary**.

Appropriate language. If you are explaining a technical matter to a lay audience, or writing an instruction manual for equipment for use by non-specialists, then use words that they are likely to know, not technical jargon. Explain any necessary terms as simply as you can, while trying not to sound patronising.

Style. One must use the **appropriate style** as well as suitable words. For example, descriptions of fast action in novels are usually given in short sentences, in short paragraphs, while philosophical discussions are often written with longer, more complicated sentences and longer paragraphs. **Specialised styles** are used in business correspondence (pages 184–97). In any kind of writing, use sentences which vary in length and construction to add interest and avoid monotony.

CHAPTER 4

Checking your work, with an exercise in critical reading and a vocabulary challenge

Checking your work

It is essential to **read your own work critically**, paying attention to the English as well as to the facts or message. With training, you should be able to monitor sense and English in the same reading, but if you cannot do that yet, monitor for sense first, then for English errors and style. Give checking your full 'brain-on' attention.

A **failure to check** can have serious consequences or be very embarrassing, as shown by these examples. A man wrote to a publisher, asking for a job as a proof-reader, and proof-readers have to be experts at spotting errors. He was unsuccessful as his letter asked for a job as a *poof-reader*! A research student who failed to check her PhD thesis properly was asked by the external examiner to make 180 changes, by hand, to three copies of her thesis.

A recent book on the spirit of the ancient Chinese began with the word *Introdcution*. A print run of a Penguin book was pulped because *Pengiun* was on the title page. The CEO of an American cancer-treatment machine firm showed a slide

'Introdcution' – he failed to check!

giving his firm's number of employees as 450 and the company's annual income as $233.6, presumably omitting 'million', a huge difference.

Checking was lacking from *The Daily Telegraph Sport* (12/12/2009). An article about Olympic swimmer Rebecca Adlington had a photo with the bizarre caption: **'Caption Nfficicis niii tiii Biiitish-bcckxd Siiirrc Liiinx'**.

The same newspaper (29/1/2010) had a classic example of a failure to check for common sense:

> *I couldn't believe it when they sent me an email telling me that my Dad's Army board game could insight violence and hatred . . .*

Incite and *insight* are pronounced the same but with totally different meanings.

Checking one's own work critically should be routine. Sometimes one has omitted an important word such as *not*, or put in the wrong word, or written an incomplete sentence, or omitted an important idea which had been in one's mind but did not make it into writing. Our brains occasionally supply a missing word when we read a piece through, and may do so repeatedly.

For **really important documents**, such as CVs, job application letters and contracts, it is best to get a friend or colleague to read them through with a fresh pair of eyes. When my wife reads one of my pieces, she often spots mistakes which I missed even in several re-readings. An eminent colleague at work was embarrassed by mistakes he had made in setting a final-degree exam paper, so he started sending me draft papers to check for English and sense.

Somerset Maugham, in *Of Human Bondage*, wrote: '*People ask you for criticism, but they only want praise.*' While that is mainly true, it is helpful to get other people's opinions on your writing, even if you disagree with their comments. Their views can stimulate new ideas and help you to correct errors, inconsistencies or passages which do not read smoothly.

Some people can check well on a **computer screen**, aided by the word-processor's **underlining** of what might be errors in various colours from built-in grammar- and spell-checkers. Others prefer to check a **printed** version.

For a **word-processed document**, a good combination is to check on screen any of those warning underlinings, and then check a printed version. **Grammar-checkers** and **spell-checkers** are much improved compared with ones from ten years ago, but are not infallible, so use your judgement in whether to make any changes in response to them. There are text-to-voice computer programs which read the text back aloud, when certain errors and omissions can be detected as the sentences sound wrong.

Exercise in critical reading and error-spotting

When you feel that something is wrong in the following piece, in spelling, grammar, punctuation, word choice or consistency, please note it down. You can compare your list of errors with the one given later (pages 37–8) where each error is explained. Some errors should be obvious but others are more subtle.

It is raining as Sargeant Greene-Thomson begins to lead his soldiers into the at tack on the enemies out-post. The men, who's bravery was unquestionible, were lead behind the farmhouses cowshed. Its true that they were inwardly frightened, but they did'nt let it show.

'Hey, Sarge. Did you hear that?" wispered private Higgs. 'Over their. Behind those trees. A low whaling, mowning sound, like a ghost. It's to spookey.'

An owl flue low over his head and hooted loud.

Frightening the highly tense soldiers quite badly.

'Quiet, Higgs, or the enemy will here us. Lets see if their coming closer. Have you're guns ready, men.'

They waited for what seamed an age, one of the men sneezed, spoiling any chance of surprising their foes. Because the noise and hooting had effected their nerves; the men were jumpy. Sergent Green-Thompson finaly decided to re-treat and regroup. He gestured to the soldiers to go back passed the farm house and it's cowshed, and then slowly walk back to bass. This was just tempory accomodation in a barn.

Read the passage again, slowly. You may discover more errors – there are about forty of them. Try to explain to yourself why each mistake is wrong, although you should be able to do so much better after reading the appropriate sections of this book.

Vocabulary challenge

Having a large vocabulary is so useful in understanding the words of others, and in selecting the right word for what you want to write or say. English has a huge and fascinating vocabulary. The words in this challenge have been chosen as those which many readers will know and others might not, excluding really common words.

Check whether you know a word well enough to explain its meaning to someone who does not know it at all. Consult a dictionary if necessary.

Brief definitions are given later but are not complete. Most words in a dictionary have more than one meaning and all the alternatives cannot be given here.

There is a mixture of single words, short phrases, and two or more words with a slash or solidus [/] between them. In the last case, think about the differences in meaning between them. For example, with *prognosis/diagnosis*, the *diagnosis* is the assessment of what the problem is (e.g., the disease or the trouble with an organisation), while the *prognosis* is the forecast of the likely outcome over time. If the diagnosis is lung cancer, the prognosis might be death within six months unless the tumour is treated.

Taking the vocabulary challenge on your own is fine but it is more fun to do it with others with whom you can discuss your answers.

- acme
- androgynous
- antediluvian
- archetype
- attenuation
- bowdlerised
- caesura
- coincide
- cornucopia
- diurnal
- epistolatory
- erudition
- expletive
- fissiparous
- heuristic
- hyperbole
- impugn
- kleptomaniac
- laudatory
- matrilineal
- adipose
- anodyne
- anthropomorphism
- arrogate
- avuncular
- buss
- cerebrate
- collocation
- corpulent
- effulgent
- epitome
- exegesis
- farinaceous
- fractious
- homogenisation
- hyperthermia
- interdict
- lambent
- malleable
- monoglot

- neonatal
- oenophile
- orotund
- oxymoron
- persiflage
- pleonastic
- predation
- prolix
- riparian
- ruminant
- scintillating
- symposium
- theocracy

- nuance
- oleaginous
- overt
- patricide
- photochromic
- postprandial
- preternatural
- pyromaniac
- rubicund
- schism
- sinistral
- tendentious

- acrophobia/agoraphobia
- annual/annular
- bovine/ovine/porcine
- comestible/combustible
- cosseted/corseted
- erroneous/erogenous
- extra marital/extra-marital
- hoar/haw/whore
- lapsed/prolapsed
- mooted/muted
- prodigal/prodigious
- rational/rationale
- secret/secrete
- suit/suite

- advent/Advent
- axillary/auxiliary
- canned/caned
- corolla/corollary
- dissemble/disassemble
- erupt/eruct
- fortuitous/fortunate
- humorous/humerus
- meter/metre
- mural/murine/marine
- radiate/irradiate
- sacrum/sacristan
- senile/sessile
- volt/vault

Answers to error-spotting

As most of the piece is in the past tense, both verbs in the first sentence should be in the past tense. The two different spellings of *Sergeant* are wrong. *Attack* should not have a space between *at* and *tack*. *Enemies* is possessive and should be *enemy's*. *Outpost* should not be hyphenated. *Who's* should be *whose*. *Unquestionable*, not *-ible*. Were *led*, not *lead*. *Farmhouse's*. *Its true* should be *It's true*, short for *It is true*. *Did'nt* should be *didn't*, as the omitted letter is the *o* of *not*.

The first spoken piece – 'Hey, Sarge. Did you hear that?" *wispered private Higgs*, starts with a single quotation mark ['] and ends with a double quotation mark ["]. Either is correct, but a writer must be consistent within a piece. *Whispered* needs that *h*, and *private* should be *Private*, as it is his title. *Over their* should be *over there*; the sound was more likely to be *wailing* than *whaling*. *Mowning* should be *moaning*, *to* should be *too*, and *spooky* is not spelled *spookey*.

The owl *flew*, not *flue*. The way it hooted needs the adverb *loudly*, not the adjective *loud*. The next part, *Frightening . . . quite badly*, is an incomplete sentence as it lacks a subject and main verb; *frightening* is a present participle, not a finite verb (see pages 55–7). There are a number of spoken short incomplete sentences, but that often happens in normal speech. *The enemy will hear us*, not *here*. *Lets* should be *let's* (let us); *if their* should be *if they're*. *You're* is short for *you are*; it should be *your guns*.

Seamed should be *seemed*. The sentence, *They waited for what seamed an age, one of the men sneezed, spoiling any chance of surprising their foes*, is made up of two complete sentences, each with its own subject and finite verb; it is an example of run-on sentences, a comma splice (page 70). It should be two separate sentences, or they should be connected, for example, by putting *then* after the first comma. Their nerves had been *affected*, not *effected* (which means *accomplished*). The semicolon after *nerves* is wrong, interrupting the flow of meaning; it should be a comma.

The name *Greene-Thomson* has two changes, to *Green-Thompson*. *Finaly* is made up of the adjective *final* and the suffix *-ly*, so it has a double *l*. *Re-treat* means to treat again, so should have no hyphen when meaning *go back*. *Passed* should be *past*. While *farm house* and *farmhouse* are both permissible, one should be consistent here. *It's cowshed* should be *its cowshed*. *Bass* should be *base*; *tempory* should be *temporary* and *accomodation* needs a double *m*.

Most of the points and grammatical terms are explained in detail elsewhere in this book.

Answers to the vocabulary challenge

These short definitions are not complete and do not cover all meanings of a particular word. They are given very briefly, in incomplete English, to save space.

Acme, summit of achievement; *adipose*, relating to fat; *androgynous*, having a mixture of male and female characteristics; *anodyne*, something relieving pain and distress, soothing, bland; *antediluvian*, old-fashioned, before the biblical flood; *anthropomorphism*, attributing human characteristics to animals; *archetype*, original or perfect model; *arrogate*, to claim or seize without justification; *attenuation*, weakening, reduction; *avuncular*, friendly, like an uncle.

Bowdlerised, removed the sexy bits from a play or book; *buss*, kiss; *caesura*, a pause in a line of verse; *cerebrate*, think, ponder; *coincide*, occur together; *collocation*, grouping together, as of words near each other; *cornucopia*, horn of plenty, abundant source; *corpulent*, bulky, fat; *diurnal*, occurring in the day; *effulgent*, brilliant, shining; *epistolatory*, conducted by, or consisting of, letters; *epitome*, typical example, embodiment; *erudition*, great learning; *exegesis*, important explanation or study; *expletive*, swear word.

Farinaceous, starchy, as of foods; *fissiparous*, divisive; *fractious*, bad-tempered, irritable; *heuristic*, helping to learn or teach; *homogenisation*, blending, making uniform, breaking up particles; *hyperbole*, exaggeration; *hyperthermia*, having a high, feverish temperature; *impugn*, denigrate; *interdict*, forbid, prevent; *kleptomaniac*, someone with a pathological urge to steal; *lambent*, glowing or licking; *laudatory*, expressing praise.

Malleable, able to be beaten, bent or moulded into shape, able to be influenced; *matrilineal*, relating to descent through the female line; *monoglot*, knowing only one language; *neonatal*, relating to the newborn; *nuance*, subtle difference; *oenophile*, wine lover; *oleaginous*, oily in character; *orotund*, pompously spoken, booming; *overt*, open, not hidden; *oxymoron*, a combination of contradictory terms, e.g., *a smart dumb blonde*.

Patricide, murder of one's father, or the person doing that; *persiflage*, flippant banter, teasing; *photochromic*, darkening in brighter light, like some sunglasses; *pleonastic*, redundant (of words); *postprandial*, after lunch or dinner; *predation*, the killing and eating of one animal species by another; *preternatural*, supernatural, abnormal; *prolix*, wordy, verbose; *pyromaniac*, one with a pathological urge to start fires.

Riparian, relating to river banks; *rubicund*, ruddy, reddish; *ruminant*, animal having a four-chambered stomach and chewing the cud; *schism*, division into opposing groups; *scintillating*, sparkling, lively, brilliant; *sinistral*, relating to the left side; *symposium*, a conference or a collection of scholarly papers; *tendentious*, biased in assumption, presumptuous; *theocracy*, government by the priesthood or a god.

Acrophobia, a fear of heights/*agoraphobia*, a fear of public or open spaces; *advent*, arrival or coming/*Advent*, the period before Christmas; *annual*, occurring once a year/*annular*, ring-like; *axillary*, relating to the armpit or plant axils/*auxiliary*, helping, secondary; *bovine/ovine/porcine*, respectively relating to cattle, sheep and pigs; *canned*, put in cans/*caned*, beaten with a cane; *comestible*, food/*combustible*, capable of being burnt; *corolla*, the petals of a flower/*corollary*, a natural result or obvious deduction; *cosseted*, pampered, cared for well/*corseted*, wearing a corset.

Dissemble, try to deceive, to conceal/*disassemble*, take apart; *erroneous*, faulty/*erogenous*, sensitive to sexual stimulation; *erupt*, break out, eject volcanic matter, show sudden anger/*eruct*, burp; *extra marital*, additional within marriage/*extra-marital*, outside marriage; *fortuitous*, accidental, by chance/*fortunate*, lucky.

Hoar, a kind of frost/*haw*, fruit of the hawthorn/*whore*, prostitute; *humorous*, funny/*humerus*, bone of the upper arm; *lapsed*, expired, or no longer following something/*prolapsed*, fallen, sunken, used of a womb; *meter*, measuring device/*metre*, 100 cm, or poetic rhythm; *mooted*, suggested/*muted*, quietened or silenced; *mural*, wall painting/*murine*, relating to mice and rats/*marine*, relating to the sea.

Prodigal, wasteful, lavish/*prodigious*, astonishing, large, powerful; *radiate*, emit radiation or spread out/*irradiate*, to subject to radiation; *rational*, logical, sensible/*rationale*, the reason behind something; *sacrum*, five fused vertebrae in the lower back/ *sacristan*, person in charge of church items; *secret*, kept hidden or private/*secrete*, make and release a secretion; *senile*, relating to old age and its weaknesses/*sessile*, permanently attached to a surface, not motile; *suit*, set of clothes or cards/*suite*, a set of furniture, or several attendants; *volt*, unit of electrical potential/ *vault*, underground chamber or arched structure, storage facility, to jump over.

CHAPTER 5

A quick look at essential English language terms

We need to look at some essential words in order to understand how faults in English arise, and how to spot and rectify them. Most of the words are dealt with in more detail later. Even if you hated grammar at school, or never did it, or have forgotten it, you should find this chapter painless and helpful.

Consider this sentence:

Jack offered her a shiny gold ring, and she accepted it immediately.

This is a **sentence**, making sense on its own, starting with a capital letter and ending in a full stop. It is a **compound sentence**, made up of two **simple sentences** joined by the **conjunction** *and*:

Jack offered her a shiny gold ring. [and] She accepted it immediately.

Each sentence is grammatically complete, with a **subject** (*Jack, She*) and a **finite verb** (*offered, accepted*) in the past tense. A verb is in its finite (limited) sense when it is limited by having a specific tense and person (such as first person *I offered*, or third person, *he offered*). A verb in the infinitive, such as *to offer*, is not limited by tense or person. A **participle**, such as *offering*, is not a finite verb: it has no person. Suppose we just had:

Offering her a shiny gold ring.

That is not a complete sentence as it has no subject and no finite verb, just a present participle, *offering*. **Incomplete sentences** are very common, and wrong.

In *Jack offered her a shiny gold ring*, there are two **nouns**, or naming words. One names *Jack* and one names a *ring*. *Jack* is a **proper noun**, naming a unique person, and is always spelled with an initial capital letter. In contrast, *ring* is a **common noun** and does not have an initial capital letter unless it starts a sentence.

In *She accepted it immediately*, the subject *She* is a **pronoun**, standing in for a noun. From this fragment, we cannot tell what her name is.

Verbs are words indicating action, such as *offered*, or they indicate states of being (with the verb *to be*), or having, feeling, seeming, etc. They can be finite, with a subject, number (singular or plural), tense, voice and mood, or can be in the infinitive. Their **voice** can be **active** (*he hit her*) or **passive** (*she was hit*). They can be **transitive**, taking a **direct object** which receives the action, so *hit* here is a transitive verb, subject *he*, direct object *her*. Verbs can be intransitive, with no object receiving the action, as in *He meditated*. There may be an **indirect object**. In *She threw her shoe at him*, what she threw was her shoe, the direct object, and what she threw it at is the indirect object, *him*.

The **mood** of a verb can be **indicative**, as in a statement, **imperative**, as in a command, or **subjunctive**, expressing doubt or supposition.

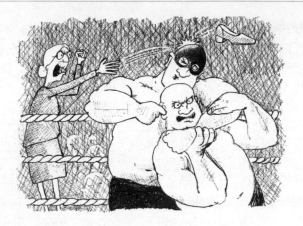

She threw her shoe at him.

Some verbs are called **auxiliary verbs**, meaning 'helping verbs'. Although they can function as main verbs, when they function as auxiliaries they combine with other verbs to form tenses, moods and voices. They include *to be*, *to have*, *to do*, *can* (part of the verb *to be able* and lacking its own infinitive), *will* (also lacking an infinitive in the auxiliary sense). For example, combined with parts of the verb *to go*, we get combinations such as *will go* (future), *did go* (past), *have gone* (past).

Nouns may be modified by descriptive **adjectives**. In the first sentence on page 42, the noun *ring* is modified by two adjectives, *shiny* and *gold*. It was not just any old ring; it was a shiny gold one. *Gold* is sometimes a noun but here is an adjective: this illustrates that the same word can be more than one **part of speech**. The **main parts of speech** are nouns, pronouns, verbs, adjectives, adverbs, conjunctions, prepositions and interjections.

Adverbs qualify verbs (and adjectives and adverbs), telling us more about what happened. In *She accepted it immediately*, the **adverb** *immediately* tells us when she accepted the ring.

Prepositions, as the name suggests, usually occur before the noun or pronoun to which they apply, relating that word to some other part of the sentence. Examples include *at, for, from, in, on, to, up* and *upon*. In *She threw her shoe **at** him*, *at* is the preposition, relating to the following pronoun, *him*.

Conjunctions join words, phrases or sentences. They include *and, but, or, although, because, if* and *since*. For example: *Jack **and** Jennifer, **but** not Toby **or** Jill, went by train, **although** it was expensive*.

Interjections are exclamations which often have little grammatical relation to the rest of the sentence, or which are on their own. They can be single words or phrases. Examples include *my goodness, oh, alas, blast* and various swear words. They are often followed by exclamation marks: *Damn! I forgot my wallet*.

Phrases are groups of related words at a level between single words and clauses, lacking a finite verb, while **clauses** are groups of words including a subject and a finite verb, but not necessarily making a complete sentence. We previously considered the sentence *Jack offered her a shiny gold ring, and she accepted it immediately*. Here we have two clauses linked by the conjunction *and*. *Jack offered her a shiny gold ring* is one clause, containing a subject and a finite verb, and *she accepted it immediately* is another clause, also containing a subject and a finite verb. The words *a shiny gold ring* make a noun phrase, not a clause, as there is no finite verb.

Other **types of phrase** include adjectival, adverbial, prepositional and verbal. For example, in *He bowled very quickly and accurately*, the words *very quickly and accurately* describe how he bowled and make an adverbial phrase.

There are **two types of clause**: **main clauses** make complete sense on their own, while **subordinate clauses** do not, depending on a main clause to complete their sense:

We went to the café because we were hungry.

The main clause is *We went to the café*, which makes sense on its own. The subordinate clause, *because we were hungry*, explains why we went to the café, but does not make sense on its own.

CHAPTER 6

Be versatile with verbs

🌿 Introduction

Verbs describe **actions**: *He wrestled with the crocodile*, or describe **states of being**: *He was afraid*. Verbs describing states of being, such as *be*, *seem*, *know* and *want*, are called **stative** verbs, while action verbs such as *throw* and *hold* are called **nonstative**.

Many **sentence errors** come from having no finite verb, just participles, or from having hanging participles: see page 57. An extremely common error is to use a **singular verb with a compound subject**, where two singular subjects are connected by *and*. *Agriculture and industry is very important to this country* – a correct sentiment but grammatically wrong. In maths, $1 + 1 = 2$, so in grammar two single subjects make a plural subject.

Getting the forms of a verb wrong usually shows ignorance but has been used to indicate that a fictional character is simple or juvenile, and for humour. Bluebottle in *The Goon Show* was a naïve character. He used wrong verb forms such as *He falled in the water* and *He hitted me*; those verbs are irregular (past tenses *fell* and *hit*) but have been treated as if regular. He also used some wrong verbs, as in *He deaded me*, instead of *killed*.

- With verbs, you can show person, tense, voice and mood.
- Verbs can inflect (change) in regular or irregular ways.
- They must **agree in number** (singular or plural) with their subject.

Verbs can be in the **infinitive**, e.g., *to go, to hate,* where they are not limited by tense, person, number, voice or mood (see below). In contrast, a **finite form** of a verb is limited by those attributes: [he] *goes;* [we] *went;* [she] *was punched; punch!*

Verbs can be **transitive**, with the action transferred from the subject to the object, or **intransitive**, where there is no object. Some verbs are transitive in some uses and intransitive in others.

Here the verbs are **transitive**:

The bull charged the farmer.

He wrote a poem.

The Arctic cold froze his nose.

The bull charged the farmer.

48

Here the verbs are **intransitive**:

He meditated.

She sneezed.

They froze at the sound of the sentry.

Thus *froze* is transitive in one sentence with the object *his nose* but intransitive in *they froze*. Some verbs are usually transitive, e.g., *distract, find, close*; some are usually intransitive, e.g., *arrive, sneeze, meditate, die*, and some may be either, e.g., *pause, cook*. There is a tendency to blur the difference between transitive and intransitive verbs. My dictionary lists *to enjoy* as transitive; it takes a direct object as one enjoys something. Restaurant staff often say '*Enjoy*' as they serve the food, as if the verb were intransitive.

Person

Person indicates the kind of subject which a verb has. Verbs can be in the **first person** (*I* or *we* as the subject), **second person** (*you*, singular or plural) or **third person** (*he, she* or *it, they* or a *noun*). A regular verb **conjugates** (changes) as follows in the present tense:

Singular: *I punch, you punch, he, she* or *it* (or a noun, such as *the kangaroo*) *punches*.

Plural: *we punch, you punch, they* (or a plural noun, such as *the kangaroos*) *punch*.

The only inflection in the present tense is in the third person singular. In the past tense, there is no inflection:

I, you, he, she, it, the kangaroo, we, you, they, the kangaroos punched.

✿ Tense

Tense indicates the time of action or state of being, such as present, past or future. In the example of *punch* (present tense), *punched*, the *-ed* ending of *punched* shows that that is the past tense. In some **irregular verbs**, the **present** and **past** tenses are the same, as in *read, read* and *hit, hit*, which is confusing. It is much more important to be able to use different tenses accurately than to know their grammatical names.

Each verb on its own has only two tenses, **present** and **past**, as in *punch, punched*, but we can make other tenses such as the **future** by using **auxiliary (helping) verbs**, such as *will, shall, have, am, do, go*. With auxiliary verbs we can make a distinction between the present and past tenses of *hit: I am hitting; I was hitting*.

Grammarians differ as to how many tenses there are in English and as to what they should be called. The main ones are the **present, past** and **future**, but these can be subdivided. These **subdivisions** enable us to specify exactly what the action or situation is, was or will be. They are the **simple, continuous, perfect** and **perfect continuous tenses**. Do not be put off by the terminology as the examples will make everything clear. Think of 'perfect' as meaning finished, completed (perfected).

PRESENT AND PAST TENSES

The **simple tense** consists of a single word and is sometimes called the *indefinite*, as it is not clear whether the action has finished: **present simple**, *I punch*; **past simple**, *I punched*. The simple tense is considered indefinite as it could be a single action: *I punched John once on the jaw* or a continuing one: *I punched John for several minutes.*

The **continuous tense** uses auxiliary verbs to show that the action is still continuing: **present continuous**, *I am punching*; **past continuous**, *I was punching.* The same idea can be conveyed by the simple and by the continuous tense, as in *I drew the nude model for three hours* or *I was drawing the nude model for three hours.*

Next we have the **perfect tense**, also using auxiliary verbs, where the action has stopped: **present perfect**, *I have punched* (note the present tense of the auxiliary verb, *have*); **past perfect**, *I had punched* (past tense of the auxiliary verb, *had*).

In the **perfect continuous tenses**, the action had been continuing before it stopped: **present perfect continuous**, *I have been punching*; **past perfect continuous**, *I had been punching.*

These distinctions affect the meaning in various forms of the **past tense**:

I punched him when the police arrived. I did not punch him until the police arrived – past simple.

I was punching him when the police arrived. The police arrived as I was punching him – past continuous.

I had punched him when the police arrived. I had punched him, perhaps only once, when the police arrived – past perfect.

I had been punching him when the police arrived. I had been punching him for a time when the police arrived – past perfect continuous.

THE FUTURE TENSE

We have to use auxiliary verbs, especially *shall* and *will*, to make the **future tense**, which can be subdivided.

In the **indefinite future**, it is not clear whether the action will have finished: *I will punch.*

The action continues in the **continuous future**: *I will be punching.*

In the **perfect future**, the action will have finished: *I will have punched.*

In the **perfect continuous future**, the action will have been continuous but will have finished: *I will have been punching.*

OTHER TIME INDICATIONS

There are other ways of **writing about future events**, involving auxiliary verbs, including *going*.

> *I am meeting Rebecca tomorrow.*

> *I will be meeting Rebecca tomorrow.*

> *I am going to meet Rebecca tomorrow.*

Curiously, one can use the present continuous tense to indicate the present or the future:

> *'Right now I am cooking lunch for the family.'* [Present]

> *'I am cooking lunch for the family next Sunday.'* [Future]

Voice

Verbs conveying action can be in the **active voice**, where the subject does something to a direct object, or in the **passive voice**, where the action is done **to** the subject, not **by** the subject.

These examples show the **active voice**:

> *James swindled Robert.*

> *The farmer milks the cow.*

> *She had painted a portrait.*

These examples show the **passive voice**:

> *Robert was swindled by James.*

> *The cow is milked by the farmer.*

> *The portrait had been painted by her.*

Note the use of the auxiliary verb *to be* in the passive voice: *was*, *is*, *had been*, in those examples.

Use the active or passive voice according to your inclination or the context. In a fast-moving passage in a novel, the active voice is more suitable than the passive voice: *The gangster shot him dead*, rather than *He was shot dead by the gangster*.

In science, we were told always to use the passive voice: *The solution was heated to 60°C*, or *The rabbit's breathing was studied at different oxygen concentrations*. There is now more encouragement of the active voice: *We heated the solution to 60°C*, or *I studied the rabbit's breathing at different oxygen concentrations*.

If writing for any academic journal, see what its policy is on active or passive voices, checking published articles there. However, one does not want to overuse the pronouns *I* or *we* if using the active voice to report experiments.

✑ Mood

Verbs have three **moods**: **indicative**, **imperative** and **subjunctive**. The **indicative mood** is used for normal statements and questions:

I owe John money.

The train was late.

What is your motive?

The **imperative mood** involves orders, whether abrupt or polite, and usually with the understood subject, *you*:

Go to hell!

Keep off the grass.

Please fetch me another beer.

The **subjunctive mood** is less obvious, but anyone who has heard the carol or read Christina Rossetti's poem 'Mid-Winter' will have met the lines:

If I were a shepherd
I would bring a lamb,
If I were a wise man
I would do my part.

The speaker was not a shepherd or a wise man, so did not use the indicative mood, *I was*. Instead, the writer used the **subjunctive** because this is **supposition** of what he or she would do **if** he or she were a shepherd or a wise man. Note the word *if*, followed by the subjunctive.

The subjunctive is used for **uncertain situations** such as hypotheses, suppositions, wishes, hopes, imaginings, doubts and proposals. *If* may signal the subjunctive, as may the verb forms *may, be, were*. The subjunctive can be recognised if the verb form differs from that of the indicative. This happens in the present tense, third person, which does not have the 's' ending in the subjunctive, and the verb *to be* is just *be* for all persons, instead of *is, am, are*. In the past subjunctive, *were* is used for all persons of the verb *to be* (e.g., I *were*, not I *was*). Here are some examples of the subjunctive mood:

May you be happy always. [A wish or hope]

She wishes that she were taller. [Wish]

If I were you, I would accept today. [Supposition, implying *Suppose that I were you.*]

He proposed that she go skiing with him. [Proposal; *go*, not *goes*]

Imagine if I were king and you were my queen. [Imagination]

Do not use the subjunctive for factual statements:

*When I **was** young, I did not chat up girls.*

When it is supposition, imagination or hypothesis, use the subjunctive:

*If I **were** young again, I would chat up girls.*

Participles

Verbs have **participles**, such as *snowing*, the present participle of *to snow*, with *snowed* as the past participle. They are called participles because they take part in forming verbs when used with auxiliary verbs, as in *It has snowed*. On their own, **participles**

are not finite verbs; they have a tense but not person, number, voice or mood.

Present participles usually end in *-ing*, e.g., *drinking, being*, coming from the present continuous tense without the auxiliary verb *to be*. They are used in all continuous tenses, including the past continuous tense, *It was snowing. I am drinking* gives us the present participle *drinking*, and *I am being* gives us *being*.

The **past participle** can be obtained from the past perfect without the auxiliary verb *to have*. Thus *I had drunk* gives the past participle *drunk*. Many past participles end in *-ed* if from regular verbs, as in *looked, mated* and *passed*, while some end in *-en*, as in *been, written* and *frozen*. The most frequent endings of past participles are *-ed, -d, -t* (*burnt*), *-en* or *-n*, but there are others: *dug, gone*.

The present and past participles can be used as **adjectives**: *his* **biting** *sarcasm*; *her* **broken** *pen*.

The present participle can be used as a **noun**, when it is called a **gerund**; it can have an article or an adjective before it. *The* **running** *of the deer* . . . ; *their silly* **giggling** . . . One should use a **possessive adjective**, not a pronoun, before a gerund: *The committee praised* **his** *braving the danger*, not *The committee praised* **him** *braving the danger*.

Many **sentence errors** come from incomplete sentences which have no finite verb, often with just a participle, e.g., *Identifying racial origins from sequencing a person's DNA.* That has two present participles but no finite verb. What should be one sentence is often split into a sentence and a sentence fragment with no finite verb: *He spent ages reading his newspaper on Sundays.* **Looking to see the Premier League and Championship football results.**

The hanging or dangling participle, with no finite verb or subject, causes frequent and sometimes amusing errors.

Looking down the microscope, the water fleas performed a dance-like movement. No; the water fleas were not looking down the microscope.

Driving my Ferrari at 90 miles an hour, the rabbit stood no chance. The rabbit was not driving the car.

✂ Phrasal verbs

A **phrasal verb** is a **multiword combination** of a verb with one or more adverbs or prepositions, or sometimes both, making a complete unit of sense. The meaning may differ from that of its component parts, e.g., *to take in*, meaning *to deceive*; *to push off*, meaning to go away (intransitive) rather than to push away (transitive); *to get over*, meaning to recover from; *to look up*, meaning *to check or research*.

It is sometimes said that one should not end sentences with prepositions, since prepositions normally come before nouns, as suggested by 'pre-position'. There are many cases where ending sentences with prepositions is completely acceptable, especially where the preposition is part of a phrasal verb:

> *Fed up with the prolonged discussion, Bert **pushed off**.*

> *Because of Fred's cunning lies, Jane was completely **taken in**.*

> *The country's prospects are **looking up**.*

Sir Winston Churchill is said to have mocked the clumsy avoidance of ending sentences with prepositions by writing:

> *This is the sort of English up with which I will not put.*

To put up with is a phrasal verb including two prepositions, normally followed by the object case, as in *I put up with him*.

Agreement in number between verb and subject

Words that come between a subject and its verb do not affect the agreement between that verb and its subject: *The **teacher** of the worst pupils in the most dilapidated classrooms **was** brilliant.*

A **compound subject** consisting of two singular nouns joined by *and* should have a plural verb: *Physics and chemistry **are** sometimes considered difficult.* Exceptions are made when certain classic combinations are treated as one single unit:

> *Whisky and soda is refreshing.*

> *Bread and butter is a tea-time staple.*

> *Health and safety is important.*

Compound subjects grouped together by **each** or **every** are considered singular:

> *Every thief, swindler and murderer in this town **is** afraid of our 'zero tolerance' policy.*

> *Each man, woman and child **is** afraid of the overhanging rock.*

With constructions involving **either . . . or**, or **neither . . . nor**, use a singular verb if both nouns are singular and a plural verb if both are plural.

> *Either Joe or Peter **is** going to drive you there; neither Elaine nor Amy **is** free then.*

> *Neither bananas nor apples **are** for long keeping.*

If one noun is singular and the other is plural, make the verb agree with whichever noun it immediately follows: *Either one mango or three bananas **are** enough for a light meal. Either three bananas or one mango **is** enough for a light meal.*

See pages 73 and 76 for subject/verb agreement for collective nouns and cases such as *one in ten is . . .*

Regular and irregular verbs

For **regular verbs**, the third person singular present tense has *-s* added to the infinitive stem, *to jump, he jumps*, while verbs ending in *s, x, z, ch* or *sh* add *-es, to push, he pushes*. To the stem of the infinitive (without the word *to*), one adds *-ed* to form the past tense and the past participle, *he pushed, pushed*, and one adds *-ing* to form the present participle, *pushing*. If the infinitive ends in a consonant followed by 'e', one removes the 'e' before adding *-ed* or *-ing, to date, dated, dating*.

Most auxiliary verbs are **irregular**, with more inflections than regular verbs, or different ways of forming past participles, e.g., *I*

am, you are, he is, we are, they are; do, did, done; can, could.
If you have doubts about whether a verb is irregular and how it
varies, consult a dictionary.

A good dictionary lists the third person singular of the
present tense, the present participle, the past tense, and the past
participle if different from the past tense, and other irregularities.
For example, under *do*, it should give *does, doing, did, done*; under
be, it should list other irregularities, such as the first, second and
third person singular present tense, *am, are, is.*

A strangely illogical irregularity involves the verbs **shall**
and **will**. For the **normal future tense**, the conjugation goes: *I
shall, you will, he will*. Where one wants to show **determination**,
command or **obligation**, the conjugation goes: *I will, you shall, he
shall*.

Normal future tense:

I shall go to work tomorrow as usual.

You will go to work tomorrow as usual.

Special determination or command:

*In spite of your entreaties, I **will** cross the strikers' picket line
tomorrow.*

*You **shall** marry him, even though you detest him.*

The split infinitive

When *The Daily Telegraph* published a letter in 2009 decrying the
split infinitive, two out of the three published letters of reply came
from members of the Queen's English Society defending its use in
certain circumstances. **If it sounds awkward, avoid it, but if the**

circumlocution needed to avoid the split infinitive sounds even clumsier, then split it! Split infinitives are best avoided unless there is a special reason for them. Splitting them with just an adverb is the most acceptable way, e.g., *I want to quickly check the figures*.

To split an infinitive with much more than an adverb often seems very clumsy:

> *I was about **to** just very carefully and extremely skilfully – with my new set of needles, which I bought by mail order – **stitch** up a torn dress.*

Here one might initially expect *to just* to be the verb, not *to stitch*.

Getting variety with verbs

In creative writing, you can be imaginative in your choice of verbs but if writing the minutes of a committee meeting, you are largely reporting what people said. No one expects minutes to be literary masterpieces but **varying the verbs** relieves monotony.

One could just put *said that* after each speaker's name or initials: *JV said . . . RS said . . . MM said . . . BL said . . .* It makes less boring reading if one varies the verb: *JV said . . . RS told us . . . MM commented that . . . BL explained that . . .*

Other verbs to use instead of *say*, when appropriate, include:

add	*aver*	*urge*
admit	*agree*	*imply*
offer	*opine*	*reply*
advise	*affirm*	*answer*
assert	*demand*	*enjoin*
inform	*insist*	*reckon*

rejoin	relate	remark
report	reveal	comment
declare	exclaim	enquire
mention	observe	predict
proffer	propose	request
respond	suggest	surmise
testify	venture	announce
complain	conclude	describe
estimate	indicate	maintain
point out	question	elaborate
elucidate	emphasise	pronounce
recommend	reiterate	speculate
volunteer	calculate	conjecture
contradict	acknowledge.	

Such alternatives are easily culled from a **crossword dictionary**, **synonym dictionary** or **thesaurus**. One doesn't have to use a different verb every time, but try to avoid monotony.

One can also induce variety by changing the **voice** between active and passive:

JV **discussed** the accounts and cash flow. [Active voice]

The expenditure **was listed** under six headings. [Passive voice]

One can use different **moods**, including the subjunctive:

If our balance **were to fall** below £50,000, we **would have to close** our office.

One can vary the way in which **tenses** are expressed:

We are next going to meet . . . We will next meet . . . We will next be meeting . . . We shall meet next . . . We next meet . . . We are next meeting . . .

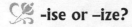 -ise or –ize?

Sometimes the endings *-ise* and *-ize* affect the meaning of verbs, as with *prise/prize*, but often they do not, as with *authorise/authorize*, both of which are correct. Which does one choose? According to Burchfield in *The New Fowler's Modern English Usage*, *-ise* is compulsory in a series of verbs of French origin, including *advise*, *arise*, *chastise*, *despise*, *exercise* and *surprise*, but in many other verbs, either form may be used. For words of Greek origin, *-ize* would better reflect their origin.

Burchfield wrote:

> *In Britain the Oxford University Press (and until recently, The Times) presents all such words with the termination spelt* -ize. *So do all American writers and publishers. It should be noted, however, that many publishing houses in Britain, including Cambridge University Press, now use* -ise *in the relevant words.*

You can make your own choice but should be consistent. I prefer *-ise* and at a Queen's English Society meeting, the informal vote was ten to one in favour of *-ise*.

And, to or with?

I am going **to try and go** *to Paris*: here *try* and *go* are not two verbs separately applying to the phrase *to Paris*. Logically, one should say: *I am going* **to try to go** *to Paris*, but this odd usage is deep-seated.

To can imply purpose while *and* implies something additional but not necessarily intentional. Compare these sentences:

63

*I went for a medical check-up **to see** a gynaecologist.*

*I went for a medical check-up **and saw** a gynaecologist.*

The latter was my experience; the doctor who saw me just happened to be a gynaecologist, whose speciality was irrelevant to me as I am a man.

To compare someone **to** something means saying how they are alike. To compare someone **with** something means saying how they are alike and unlike.

*When I compare you **to** Ghengis Khan, I find that both of you are ruthless, aggressive and successful.*

*When I compare you **with** your brother, I find that you are more intelligent but less handsome.*

CHAPTER 7

Getting the sentence right is crucial

Types of sentence

To see what common errors are made with sentences, and how to avoid and correct them, we need to look at the characteristics of sentences and learn some descriptive terms. The chapter on verbs (pages 47–64) gives important background information, as does that on grammatical terms (pages 42–6).

- A sentence is a **sequence of related words** starting with a capital letter and ending in a full stop [.] for a statement, a question mark [?] for a question, or an exclamation mark [!] for an exclamation or command.
- It is usually a **unit of complete sense**, containing a subject and a finite verb, capable of being understood on its own.
- In speech or writing, it may consist of a single word, such as 'Yes,' but the rest of the answer to the question is understood, so that 'Yes' might be short for 'Yes, I am coming now.' The subject you is understood in orders: 'Go to hell!'

Let us start with different types of sentence.

He moves.

He is the **subject** of the **verb** *moves*, which tells us what the subject is doing. It is a complete sentence, making sense on its own. It is a **simple sentence**, and the singular verb **agrees** with its singular subject.

*He moves **the piano**.*

Here there is a **direct object** of his moving, *the piano*. We can add an adverbial phrase, showing where the piano is moved to:

*He moves the piano **into the dining room**.*

This remains a simple sentence, complete in its meaning.

It seems illogical, but by adding something to a complete sentence, we can make it incomplete:

When *he moves the piano into the dining room.*

This is a **subordinate clause**, needing a **main clause** to complete it:

*When he moves the piano into the dining room, **he often hits the door frame**.*

That now makes complete sense, with a subordinate clause followed by a main one. A main clause can stand on its own but a subordinate clause cannot. A sentence containing at least one subordinate clause is called a **complex sentence**.

Subordinate clauses may come at the beginning, middle or end of complex sentences. They usually follow **subordinating conjunctions** which include *although*, *after*, *whereas*, *unless*, *since*, *because*, *when*, *while* and *if*, as in:

◄──────── SUBORDINATE CLAUSE ────────► ◄──────── MAIN CLAUSE ────────►
When Joan rejected Peter's proposal, she cast aside the proffered ring,
◄──── SUBORDINATE CLAUSE ────►
which was made of platinum.

Or they may be introduced by relative pronouns, such as *who*, *which*, *that* or *whose*, as in:

RELATIVE PRONOUN
◄──┼── SUBORDINATE CLAUSE ──►
The car **which had the racy spoiler** *was stolen.*

Compound sentences contain at least two main clauses, of equal status; they are often joined by a conjunction, a comma, a semicolon or a colon, as in:

CONJUNCTION
◄──────────── MAIN CLAUSE ────────────► │
He moves the piano into the dining room **and**
◄──────────── MAIN CLAUSE ────────────►
he turns it with its keyboard facing the window.

Each clause in a compound sentence could stand as a separate sentence, although the subject (in this case *he*) of one or more of them might be understood rather than stated:

He moved the piano into the dining room, turned it to face the window, set up his music on the stand, and played a Chopin sonata very badly.

Sequences in sentences

The commonest **sequence** in a sentence is subject, verb, then any remaining parts such as objects, but that order may be changed for specific purposes or for variety. One can invert the subject and verb in questions, so that *She is mad* becomes *Is she mad?*

Placing a word or phrase at the beginning of a sentence adds emphasis to it:

Lateness in a man was something she could never abide.

Vary your sentence structure

A succession of short, simple sentences makes boring, jerky reading, and may suggest that the writer is simple:

John likes cricket. He is mainly a batsman. Sometimes he bowls. Once he hit a big six. It broke a window in the pavilion. He had to pay for it.

This information can be given in a livelier form by joining some sentences and rewording it:

John likes cricket; although he is mainly a batsman, he also bowls. Once he hit a big six which broke the pavilion window, and he had to pay for its repair.

That has two sentences instead of six, with more variation in structure and a better flow of information. Ideally, you should aim at writing a **mixture** of simple, compound and complex sentences.

Common errors with sentences

SENTENCE FRAGMENTS WITH NO FINITE VERB OR NO SUBJECT

If what is meant to be a sentence has only an infinitive or a participle, but no finite verb with its own subject, that is wrong:

> *To go bowling in Streatham on Sunday.*

> *His driving too fast.*

A complete lack of verbs is wrong: *A stupid complaint.*

Sentence fragments lack either a finite verb or a subject, or both, and often occur next to a complete sentence to which they should be joined. The sentence fragment is shown in bold type:

> *They are filthy rich.* **Unlike us.**

That would be fine when joined:

> *They are filthy rich, unlike us.*

'SENTENCES' WITH ONLY A SUBORDINATE CLAUSE, LACKING A MAIN CLAUSE

> *When we grow old together.*

> *Because they think we are stupid.*

> *Although she had several injections of Botox.*

You should feel that something is missing from each example: the main clause is missing.

THE COMMA SPLICE (RUN-ON SENTENCES) AND PUNCTUATION FOR JOINING SENTENCES

The **comma splice** is using a comma to join two separate sentences, for example:

We were starving in the jungle, it was unbearably hot.

To join sentences, one usually needs a comma plus a conjunction, or a semicolon, or a colon:

We were starving in the jungle, and it was unbearably hot.

We were starving in the jungle; it was unbearably hot.

A colon would not be so good here as the second sentence adds to the first one rather than expanding it or explaining it. A semicolon can replace a comma and a conjunction, and can be replaced by a full stop.

A comma may be sufficient to join clauses if they are very short, or where the tone is informal, as in:

Man proposes, God disposes.

When they join two sentences to make a single sentence, words such as *however, moreover, nevertheless, consequently* and *hence* usually need a semicolon before them:

Their marriage was initially happy; however, their different personalities gradually caused friction.

CHAPTER 8

What to do with nouns and pronouns

You use **nouns** for naming things, people, places, concepts and many other items. We had a brief look earlier at nouns and pronouns (page 43). **Pronouns** stand in for nouns and can be used to avoid repetition and for brevity.

Types of noun

Proper nouns or expressions start with a capital letter and, among other things, name individuals and particular geographical features such as cities, rivers and planets, and buildings, institutions and organisations. Examples include *Janet Smith, Sydney Opera House*, the *Queen's English Society*.

Books, plays and some newspapers have the principal words in their titles treated as proper nouns: *Persuasion* by Jane Austen; *The Importance of Being Earnest*; *The Times*. Days of the week and months are proper nouns: *Wednesday, March, May*. The capital letters help to distinguish the months *March* and *May* from *to march*, or *a march*, and from the verb *may* and the flower, *may*.

We can qualify proper nouns: the *beautiful River Rhine*, but do not make plurals of them if they are unique. A reference to the *River Thames* is normally to the one which flows through London. In Britain there are several rivers named *Avon*, and in the world, many towns called *Richmond*. One could then refer to *the*

Richmonds or *the Avons*. We can refer to all of the Smith family as *the Smiths*.

Common nouns name anything other than those things named by proper nouns and do not begin with a capital letter unless they start a sentence. They are not usually unique examples of their class. Examples include a *queen*, *rubber* (the substance), a *rubber* (an eraser), *roses*, a *road*, *thought* and an *ocean*.

Common nouns are classified in two main ways: as *concrete* or *abstract* nouns, or as *count* or *uncount* nouns. These categories affect the way we treat those nouns, which is why they are mentioned here: they affect our use of English.

- **Concrete nouns** involve physical realities, anything not abstract: e.g., *mud*, *John* and *rabbit*.
- **Abstract nouns** involve the intangible, e.g., *wickedness*, *truth*, *thought*, *sleep*, *terror*.
- **Count nouns** are those which can have a number qualifying them, as in *four rubbers*, *six tigers*, *thirty mosquitoes*. They usually have different forms in the singular and plural, such as *a rubber*, *four rubbers*; *a child*, *three children*. **Count nouns in the singular need a determining word before them**, such as *a*, *the*, *this*, *that*, **but they do not need (but may have) a determiner when plural**. Thus *Worm moves slowly* sounds wrong as there is no determiner before the single count noun *worm*. However, *Worms move slowly* is fine, and so is *This worm moves slowly*.
- **Uncount nouns** include abstract nouns such as *beauty* and *poverty*, and substances such as *water*, *rubber* as a commodity, not as an eraser, and *flour*. Although the same words may have count-noun equivalents, in their uncount sense they do

not take numbers in front of them, nor can they be pluralised. In their uncount sense, they do not need a determiner: *Beauty is transitory; Truth is absolute; Rubber is used in tyres.* In their count sense, say where *beauty* means a beautiful woman, they need determiners in the singular and can have numbers and plurals: *There were six beauties present; The seven waters from different lakes tasted different.*

Collective nouns include *team, quartet, committee* and *government,* and words such as *school* when referring collectively to the pupils and staff in it. People are often confused as to whether to treat collective nouns as singular or plural: *The committee is* or *The committee are?*

This is straightforward in British English. **If the members of the group are acting individually, the collective noun takes a plural verb**, as several people make a plural subject: *The committee have gone to their various homes in the countryside.* **If, however, they are acting as one body, as is often the case, the verb should be singular**: *The committee has decided to fire you.*

In general, collective nouns take singular verbs unless 'the members of' is understood before them.

The collective noun **number** can be singular or plural, though like other collective nouns it is plural in its plural form, *numbers:*

*A number of trees **are** dying in the park*: here they are dying separately, so *number* is plural.

*The number of dying trees **is** 257*: this is a single count, taking a singular verb.

*The numbers of dying trees in successive years **were** counted*: this is more than one count, taking a plural verb.

Nouns as modifiers. Nouns can act as adjectives, when they may be called modifiers, as they modify the other noun's meaning. In *university lecturer*, the noun *university* acts as an adjective, qualifying the noun *lecturer*. Other examples include *cotton shirt* and *car wheel*.

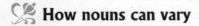 How nouns can vary

CASES

English is simpler than many foreign languages in having few **cases** for nouns. While there are six cases in Latin, English has only two for nouns: the **common case** (no separate nominative and accusative cases) and the **possessive** (genitive) **case**. The noun *assassin*, for example, stays the same whether it is a **subject**, a **direct object** or an **indirect object**, varying only in the possessive case, *assassin's*.

Subject: *The assassin threw the dagger.*

Direct object: *The wounded man punched the assassin.*

Indirect object: *The judge gave a long sentence to the assassin.*

Possessive: *The assassin's accomplice was a criminal.*

FORMING SINGULARS AND PLURALS

Most count nouns just add *-s* to **form a plural**: *boy, boys; ocean, oceans.* Some words do not have separate plurals: *cattle, series, sheep, deer, information, debris.* Some have alternative plurals: the plural of *fish* can be *fish* or *fishes; helix* can become *helixes* or *helices.*

The case of *medium* is different. *Mediums* is used for spiritualists and clairvoyants, but *media* for the press, TV and radio, and for nutrient media for growing micro-organisms. One often sees *media* treated as singular: *The media is over-influential*, but that is wrong, wrong, wrong! One even sees the false double plural: *The medias are . . .* Ugh!

Words ending in 's' may be treated as singular: *economics, physics, genetics, tennis, measles*. Words not ending in 's' may be treated as plural: *the police are . . .* Some words are always plural, e.g., *amends*. It may seem illogical but **quantities are usually treated as singular**, as if the words 'an amount of' are understood: *£300 is too much; 100 tons of concrete is arriving tomorrow.*

Words ending in *-one*, *-body* or *-thing* are normally singular, and so is *each*. *Everybody is here now. Each is entitled to his or her opinion.*

There are many other ways of forming plurals. They depend on the word's ending and the language it comes from. Most nouns ending in *s, x, z, ch* or *sh* add 'es' to form the plural: *loss, losses; sex, sexes; waltz, waltzes; church, churches; splash, splashes. Quiz* becomes *quizzes*.

Nouns ending in a consonant followed by 'y' have *-ies* plurals, changing the 'y' to 'i' and adding 'es': *economy, economies; enemy, enemies*. Words ending in a vowel plus 'y' just add 's': *monkey, monkeys; Sunday, Sundays*. Words ending in *-o* usually add 'es': *potato, potatoes; tomato, tomatoes; mosquito, mosquitoes*. Some words have unusual plurals: *goose, geese; mouse, mice; basis, bases; crisis, crises; child, children; ox, oxen; foot, feet*.

Words with Latinate plurals cause many errors. Note the following: *bacterium, bacteria; fungus, fungi; alga, algae*. I cringe when I see a newspaper referring to *a bacteria* or *a fungi*.

Those glaring errors should be avoided by all. Some words can have Latinate or ordinary plurals: *stadium: stadiums* or *stadia*; *hippopotamus: hippopotamuses* or *hippopotami*.

Beware of **compound expressions** where you may have to think which word or words should be made plural: *brothers-in-law*, not *brother-in-laws*; *trades unions*, not *trade unions*.

> Would you put: *One in ten teenagers **is** . . .* or *One in ten teenagers **are** . . .?* Both have their advocates. I use *is* in such a situation because the subject of the verb is *one*, with *in ten teenagers* as an adjectival phrase.

Pronouns and determiners

Pronouns stand for nouns but do not name them.

In *Jenny and Terry bought a cat; they took it home carefully*, *they* is a pronoun standing for *Jenny and Terry*, and *it* stands for *cat*.

Examples include *I, you, him, whom, theirs*, where only 'I' is always given a capital letter.

Determiners are words going before nouns or noun phrases and which limit their meaning. They include numbers, articles and demonstrative and possessive adjectives, e.g., *three, the, this, my, whose*.

The term **antecedent** (from Latin *ante-* before, *cedere*, to go) is used for a word which goes first, and the antecedent noun usually goes before the pronoun referring to it, but that is not fixed. In the case of the pronoun *it*, there may be no antecedent noun or only a vague implication of one:

It was raining heavily.

*Salome planned a career as a stripper, based on the Dance of the Seven Veils, but **it** was a one-off event.*

The different **persons** are **first person**, *I* (singular) and *we* (plural); **second person**, *you* (singular or plural), **third person**, *he* (masculine), *she* (feminine) and *it* (neuter or inanimate). Those are all in the **subject** (nominative) **case**; there is also the **possessive case** and, unlike the situation with nouns, an **object case** (direct and indirect object, but with no difference between them).

Listing the **personal pronouns** in order of subject, possessive, determiner (possessive adjective) and object, we have:

First person singular: *I, mine, my, me.*

Second person singular and plural: *you, yours, your, you.*

Third person singular: masculine, *he, his, his, him*; feminine, *she, hers, her, her*; neuter or inanimate, *it, its, its, it.*

First person plural: *we, ours, our, us.*

Third person plural: *they, theirs, their, them.*

Here are some examples of these pronouns and determiners in use:

I own my book; it is mine, so give it to me.

She makes her clothes; they are hers, so return them to her.

We have our friends, you have yours.

Your friends all praise you.

It has its foibles, but use it for long enough and you get used to them.

The different pronouns **inflect** (change) in very different ways with case and number, as shown above. Although the word *you* can refer to one or more people, it always takes a plural verb: *You, my only friend, are invaluable.* One occasionally meets variants such as *you is* or *we be*: they are usually errors or dialect forms.

A **common fault** is to get the **case of a pronoun wrong**, especially when a pronoun follows a noun. In *Jenny and **I** swam without clothes in the river*, 'I' is in the subject case. In *The police arrested Jenny and **me***, both *Jenny* and *me* are in the object case. One could alternatively put *The police arrested **us***. The main error is to use 'I' when the pronoun is in the object case, as in *The police arrested Jenny and **I***. Wrong!

The easy way **to get the case of the pronoun right** is to think what the pronoun would be without the preceding noun. *The police arrested I* is more obviously wrong than *The police arrested Jenny and I*. If you use phrases such as *my husband and I*, do check whether it ought to be *my husband and me*:

My husband and I went to Paris.

The landlady greeted my husband and me very warmly.

Those are both correct. In sentences such as *John is richer than I*, it is easier to put the correct pronoun if one thinks of the implied verb following the pronoun: *John is richer than I **am***.

Check whether a pronoun is in the subject or object case. In *He hit the man **who** insulted him*, *who* is correct, not *whom*, as the word *who* is the subject of the verb *insulted*, not the object of the verb *hit*.

Another common error is to have **ambiguous or wrong pronoun references. A singular pronoun should refer to the most recent singular noun, and a plural pronoun to the most recent plural noun.**

He sold her a necklace and two bangles. It was very beautiful. Because the singular noun is *necklace*, *It* must refer to that, not the bangles.

The destroyer crashed into the merchant ship. It sank. Which ship sank?

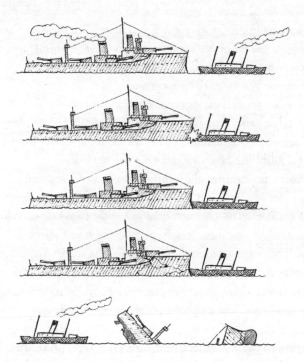

In this last example, there is ambiguity from the pronoun.

79

Possessive pronouns are often confused with contracted forms with an apostrophe and an 's', such as confusing *its* with *it's*, which is short for *it is* or *it has*. *Whose* and *theirs* are possessive and must never be confused with *who's* and *there's*, meaning *who is* or *who has*, or *there is* or *there has*. *There's a bottle of beer which is theirs. Who's asking about whose car goes fastest?*

English lacks an agreed **third person singular pronoun of common sex**, which would refer to *he* or *she*, or their derivatives. It is tedious to keep putting *he or she, his or hers, him or her*. Using *s/he* is clumsy and comes unstuck for *his or hers* or *him or her*. If you are writing instructions for a form, instead of putting *Each applicant must put his or her name*, you can use the plurals: *All applicants must put their names*. Alternatively, you can use the second person: *You must put your name*.

There are several other types of pronoun.

Reflexive pronouns include *myself, yourself, himself, herself, itself, ourselves, themselves*, as in *We shall do it ourselves*. They can be used for emphasis: *I myself will take responsibility*.

Relative pronouns relate different parts of a sentence. They include: *who* (subject), *whom* (object), *whose* (possessive), *which, that, what*, as in *The men **who** are in the rugby team, **whose** songs can be filthy, are those to **whom** your complaint should be addressed*. There is a tendency now to use *who* instead of *whom* in sentences such as *The man, who I know well, is very poorly*, when *who* is the direct object of the verb *know*. This is wrong but very common. Some people accept it, especially in speech.

Be sure to use the object case directly after a preposition: *The man **to whom** I gave money* is fine, but *The man **to who** I gave* money sounds, looks and is wrong. In discussing the target readership for a book, we would ask *Whom is it for?* because *Whom* is governed by the preposition *for*.

Interrogative pronouns help to ask questions: *who, whose, whom, which, what.*

Who is going to Glasgow today, with whom, and in whose car?

Again, do not confuse *whose* with *who's*.

Demonstrative pronouns refer to specific people or objects: *this, these* (both words often refer to nearer objects); *that, those* (often referring to more distant objects).

This is mine; would you like those?

Here *this* and *those* are demonstrative pronouns, standing for nouns which have probably been mentioned previously. The same words can also be **demonstrative adjectives**, not pronouns, as in **This** man and **those** women are Turkish.

Indefinite pronouns refer to things or people as a group or part of a group rather than individually: *each, any, some, several*. '*These peaches are delicious. I have already eaten **several**.*'

CHAPTER 9

Test yourself on nouns and pronouns

🌿 Singulars, plurals and possessives of nouns

In this list, some nouns are singular, some are plural; most are in the common case but some are in the possessive case. Keeping the original case, **change singular nouns to their plurals**, and **plural nouns to their singulars**. If no change is possible – for example, if a noun is always plural – note the fact.

Examples: church, churches; albatross's, albatrosses'; police (always treated as plural).

Test: tomato; thesis; crux; cross's; cattle; ox; brethren; foxes'; mice's; gentleman's; sheep; donkey; nappy; family's; bus; buss; fungus; virus's; bureau; château; curiosities'.

Penny; mother-in-law; colony's; maze's; death; breath; peach; pox; boxes'; bacterium; data; strata; alumni; anomaly; crisis; taxis; brother-in-law's.

Pronouns

List the personal pronouns in the subject case, in the singular, listing the person of each, e.g., I, first person. Do the same for the plurals.

Repeat this for the object and possessive cases.

What are the corresponding possessive adjectives for I, she, it, you, they, one?

What first person singular pronoun or possessive adjective should replace XXX in these sentences?

He gave John and XXX a roasting.

John and XXX hit him hard.

As I own it, it is XXX.

I can call it one of XXX possessions.

Distinguish between *their* and *they're*, and *it's* and *its*.

Answers

Tomato, tomatoes; thesis, theses; crux, cruxes; cross's, crosses'; cattle (plural only); ox, oxen; brethren, brother; foxes', fox's; mice's, mouse's; gentleman's, gentlemen's; sheep (singular and plural); donkey, donkeys; nappy, nappies; family's, families'; bus, buses; buss, busses; fungus, fungi; virus's, viruses'; bureau, bureaux;* château, châteaux;* curiosities', curiosity's.

Penny, pennies or pence; mother-in-law, mothers-in-law; colony's, colonies'; maze's, mazes'; death, deaths; breath, breaths (not breathes); peach, peaches; pox, poxes; boxes', box's; bacterium, bacteria; data, datum (the word *data* is plural); strata, stratum; alumni, alumnus (alumna is female); anomaly, anomalies; crisis, crises; taxis, taxi (cab), but there is a singular word, taxis, plural taxes, the movement of an organism in relation to a stimulus; brother-in-law's, brothers-in-law's.

*Some dictionaries allow *bureaus* and *châteaus*, but the French versions are strongly preferred.

Personal pronouns, subject case: I, first; you, second; he, she, it, third; we, first; you, second; they, third.

Object case: Me; you; him, her, it; us; you; them.

Possessive case: Mine; yours; his, hers, its; ours; yours; theirs.

Possessive adjectives: My; her; its; your; their; one's.

XXX: Me; I; mine; my.

Their = possessive adjective, third person plural, they're = they are. It's = it is or it has; its = of it.

CHAPTER 10

Qualifying with adjectives and adverbs

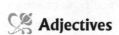 Adjectives

WHAT ADJECTIVES DO

Adjectives qualify nouns and **pronouns** only. The noun *bird* covers a huge range of birds. If we modify that with adjectives and adjectival phrases, we get something more specific: *a nocturnal, predatory, mouse-eating, hooting bird with long, tufted ears* the long-eared owl. There are single-word adjectives, such as *nocturnal*, and adjectival phrases, such as *with long, tufted ears*. Adjectives make descriptions more specific. They occasionally qualify pronouns, as in *Silly me!*

Adjectives can cause **ambiguity** when followed by more than one noun. Consider *the brown bird's nest* or *the black cab driver*. Is it the nest or the bird which is brown, or the cab or the driver which is black? We can use hyphens to resolve the ambiguity: *the brown bird's-nest* or *the brown-bird's nest*; *the black-cab driver* or *the black cab-driver*.

If you employ a **series of adjectives**, use commas between adjectives where the sense is *and*:

He was a large, fierce, beetle-browed Scotsman is equivalent to He was a large and fierce and beetle-browed Scotsman. There is no comma between the last adjective and its noun. A single adjective does not need a comma: He was a serial adulterer.

PLACING

Adjectives usually come before the noun they qualify, as in *scary face*, but they can come later, particularly after the verb *to be*: *Daniel's face was scary*.

> Adjectives can themselves be **qualified by adverbs**: *He was a **little** scared. She was **very** rich.* Here *little* and *very* are adverbs modifying the adjectives.

COMPARATIVES AND SUPERLATIVES

For short adjectives, we make the **comparative** by adding *-er* to the **absolute** (basic) form, as in *old, older*, and the **superlative** by adding *-est*: *oldest*. For a long adjective, we put the word *more* in front of it for the comparative, and *most* for the superlative: *the beautiful girl, the more beautiful girl of the two, the most beautiful girl in the school. Beautifuler* and *beautifulest* look, sound and are wrong.

Some adjectives have **irregular comparatives and superlatives**: *good, better, best; bad, worse, worst; little, less, least* (e.g., *He has little charm/less charm/the least charm*); *much, more, most; many, more, most*. Some adjectives double the final consonant before adding the suffixes for comparatives and superlatives: *thin, thinner, thinnest*. Adjectives ending in '*e*' just add *-r* or *-st*: *blue, bluer, bluest*, while those ending in *-y* change that to *-i*: *woolly, woollier, woolliest*.

TYPES OF ADJECTIVE

In English, **adjectives of nationality** have an initial capital letter: *An American city, Scotch whisky*, as do adjectives derived from proper nouns: *A Parisian café, Darwinian evolution*.

Some **demonstrative adjectives** are singular: *that book; this word*, and some are plural: *these fireworks; those rockets*. **Possessive adjectives** include: *my, your, his, her, its, our, their, one's*. **Numbers** can act as adjectives: *three hens*. **Interrogative adjectives** help one to ask questions: *Which crocodile is fiercest? What foods do they eat?*

COMPOUND ADJECTIVES

As mentioned under punctuation (page 110), **compound adjectives**, made up of more than one word, should usually be hyphenated if they apply only jointly, not separately, to the noun. In *fund-raising activities, fund-raising* is a compound adjective, with *fund* and *raising* not applying separately to *activities*. If the first word is an adverb, hyphens are not usually needed: *a very hard exam*, but *a multiple-choice question*.

UNIQUE

It is sometimes said that one should never qualify the adjective **unique** because something is or is not unique. One should never use *very unique*, but if there are very few of some object, describing them as *almost unique* is acceptable.

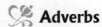 # Adverbs

Adverbs, adverbial phrases and adverbial clauses can modify verbs, adjectives and other adverbs, but not nouns and pronouns. They often **answer the questions** *How? When? Where?* or *Why?* For example:

> *Today* [when] *I kicked the ball hard* [how] *into the goalkeeper's stomach* [where; adverbial phrase] *because I disliked him* [why; adverbial clause].

Those adverbs, the adverbial phrase and the adverbial clause all modify the verb *kicked*.

Most adverbs, but not all, end in *-ly* after that has been added to the adjective: *bad, badly*; *normal, normally*, which is why *normally* has a double 'l'. In the sentence above about kicking, *hard* does not end in *-ly* but is acting as an adverb, modifying *kicked*, although it can be an adjective: *the hard problem*. Not all words ending in *-ly* are adverbs. *Anomaly* is a noun, *prickly* and *friendly* are adjectives. Do not try making such adjectives into adverbs by additions: *friendlily* looks peculiar and can be replaced by an adverbial phrase: *in a friendly fashion*.

A common fault: using adjectives instead of adverbs

You need to know which words are adjectives and which are adverbs to **avoid using adjectives where adverbs are needed**. These are wrong:

> *The medicine worked real quick.*
>
> *He painted good.*
>
> *The clock struck loud.*

The **adverbs** here should be *really* (qualifying the adverb *quickly*); *quickly*, qualifying the verb *worked*; *well*, qualifying the verb *painted*; *loudly*, qualifying the verb *struck*.

Placing that tricky word, only

Only is the most frequently misplaced word in English. It can be an adjective (*my only love*), adverb (*he cheated only once*), intensifier (*she was only too happy*) and a conjunction (*I would have hit you, only I was afraid to mark your face*). It should normally be placed directly before the word it qualifies:

> *Only I ran to the house.* The other people did not run to the house.
>
> *I only ran to the house.* I ran but did not walk, hop or skip to the house.
>
> *I ran only to the house.* I did not also run to the park or the fence.
>
> *I ran to the only house.* There were no other houses.

The placing of *only* has a fascinating **range of implications,** as shown in the exercise below. It can cause **ambiguity.** See if you detect any ambiguity here:

He only drinks port in the evening.

It could mean that he drinks nothing but port in the evening, with no whisky, beer or other drinks then, or that when he drinks port, it is only in the evening. A strict grammatical approach is that *only* qualifies the following word, the verb *drinks,* and that when he has port in the evening, he only drinks it, rather than spewing it or bathing in it. Clearly it would be better to put:

He drinks only port in the evening, or

He drinks port only in the evening.

Misplacing *only* is extremely common; in most people's speech, *only* is usually put before the verb, even when it qualifies another word. Consider:

> *I only hit her once.*

That is normal spoken English, but strictly it means that I only *hit* her, rather than *stroked*, *greeted* or *kissed* her. Technically, it should be *I hit her only once*, if that is the meaning intended. Should one be pedantic about this? As the spoken incorrect version would be widely understood with the correct meaning, I regard it as acceptable.

 Exercise (no answers are given)

Put the word *only* in all possible positions in this sentence and consider the implications:

> *The psychologist gave the baboon the banana.*

The placing of *only* has implications for the presence, absence and number of other investigators, animals and fruits, and alternatives to *gave*.

CHAPTER 11

Prepositions, articles, conjunctions and interjections

Prepositions

Prepositions are usually short words or groups of words used typically before nouns and pronouns to relate them to other parts of the sentence, showing positions, such as *on, under, up, above*. The same words can often act as adverbs, as in *He looked **up** as she climbed **down***. They are prepositions if they tell us about the following noun or pronoun, adverbs if they tell us about the verb.

In *He looked up as she climbed down the ladder*, the phrase *down the ladder* is adverbial, answering the question *Where?* in relation to the verb *climbed*, but *down* is a preposition relating to *the ladder*.

Prepositions are followed by the **object case**. This does not affect nouns but affects pronouns which have a separate object case:

*She sang to **him**.*

It is important to use the **correct preposition**. For example, there is a huge difference between *reduced **to** one tenth* and *reduced **by** one tenth*. Word confusions involving prepositions are covered on pages 167–75. The suggestion that one should never end a sentence with a preposition is refuted on pages 57–8.

People sometimes use **inappropriate prepositions**. If things differ, they differ *away* from each other; if they are similar, they are similar *towards* each other. **Different from** is logical and is preferred, while *different to* is not. *Different than* is frequent in American English. One should use *similar to*, never *similar from*. A common fault is to use **superfluous prepositions**: *I met **up with** him* is a waste of words when *I met him* is sufficient.

Articles

The **definite article**, *the*, indicates particular items (singular or plural) while the **indefinite article**, *a* and *an*, indicates something indefinite, always singular. ***The** book on the chair* is a definite book, but **A** *book on the chair* could be any book on that chair, or the only one. Articles are also called *determiners*. The rule for when nouns need a determiner was given on page 72. A common error is to put *alot* instead of *a lot* [of].

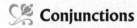 Conjunctions

TYPES AND USE

Conjunctions join words, phrases, clauses and sentences. We distinguish between **coordinating conjunctions** and **subordinating conjunctions**.

Coordinating conjunctions join parts of equal status:

*They liked bread **and** butter.*

*We went to the theatre **but** did not enjoy the play.*

*The enemy plane could be flying high **or** low.*

Where two sentences of equal status have been joined by a coordinating conjunction, they both make sense if separated:

Rufus rode a skewbald horse and Rebecca rode a palomino.

Rufus rode a skewbald horse. Rebecca rode a palomino.

Subordinating conjunctions introduce a **subordinate clause**, so that one has a **main clause** and a subordinate clause (pages 66–8). Subordinate clauses are also called **dependent clauses** as they depend on the main clause and cannot stand alone as a sentence. Subordinating conjunctions include *although, after, whereas, unless, since, because, when, while* and *if*.

*You will be in danger **if** you take that route through the jungle.*

Here the main clause is *You will be in danger*, and could stand as a separate sentence. The subordinate clause, *if you take that route through the jungle*, is introduced by the subordinating conjunction, *if*, but does not make sense on its own.

A common error is to write a subordinate clause as a complete sentence:

Whereas he preferred Sally.

Since we are going to Italy on Tuesday.

If you go down to the woods today.

None of these makes sense on its own as it is missing a main clause.

STARTING SENTENCES WITH A COORDINATING CONJUNCTION, *e.g.*, AND, BUT

This is a matter of style and choice. I avoid it unless using it for a special effect. It has been done occasionally by many excellent writers, yet why have a connector which fails to connect? It gives a jerky effect, sometimes conveying urgency, informality and matiness. Journalists do it frequently, reducing average sentence length by having two sentences rather than one longer one.

And it can certainly be overdone. An article by Gordon Brown in *The Daily Telegraph* in 2009 had nine out of thirty-one sentences starting with *And*, *But* or *So*.

Interjections

Interjections are exclamations and are often used on their own, not making complete sentences. They are frequently followed by an exclamation mark. Examples include: *Oh! Drat! Hello. Utter rubbish!* Do not copy those of the young who in speech use *like* as a meaningless interjection:

'*I'm like going on Monday to the cinema, like, with Dave.*'

95

CHAPTER 12

Using punctuation to make your meaning clear

Introduction

Punctuation standards in Britain are very low. Many people struggle with – or give up entirely on – the apostrophe, while the colon and semicolon are often missing from their repertoire, in spite of being easy to use and very helpful in constructing interesting sentences with a clear meaning. Use whatever punctuation makes the meaning clearest. Do not write

Eat brother.

if you mean

Eat, brother.

Punctuation is a set of marks which are used to separate words and groups of words to make the intended meaning clear. It can be used to emphasise words and phrases, to distinguish between major and minor ideas, and to separate groups of related words such as phrases and clauses.

Skilful punctuation is the key to good sentence construction and therefore to clear expression. It is more important **to understand how punctuation works**, by studying these examples, than to memorise long lists of all uses of all punctuation marks.

Bad punctuation can have **serious consequences**, leading to difficulties in understanding or even complete misunderstandings. Consider this sentence from the *Eastern Evening News*:

> *Don't pick up heavy weights like groceries or children with straight legs.*

That is easily misunderstood. Sensible punctuation makes it clearer:

> *Don't pick up heavy weights – like groceries or children – with straight legs.*

Putting *with your legs straight* would be better.

Bad punctuation can result in **mistaken actions**. For example, a station in East Lothian was wrongly demolished in 1984 because a comma was missing from the British Rail planning document. The list of items to preserve should have read: '*Retain Drem Station, bridge . . .*' As the comma after 'Station' was missing, the station was demolished and had to be rebuilt, although the bridge was spared.

The **amount of punctuation** a sentence requires depends on its complexity, with longer sentences usually needing more punctuation. If you are unsure of where punctuation is required, read the sentence aloud and note where your voice pauses.

Square brackets [ ] are used here to enclose examples of punctuation marks. It is helpful to know the grammatical terms which are occasionally used.

Sentence beginnings and endings

The principal unit of writing is the sentence, a group of words (occasionally just one word) which makes sense on its own, usually having a subject and a finite verb (see pages 65–70). Sentences start with a capital letter. They end with:

- a full stop [.] for statements: *'It rained.'*
- a full stop for ordinary requests: *'Please pass the salt.'*
- a full stop for mild exclamations: *'Well, we have nearly won.'*
- a question mark [?] for questions: *'Are you hungry?'*
- an exclamation mark [!] for strong exclamations: *'What a disaster!'*
- an exclamation mark for strong commands: *'Get out of my sight!'*

The main punctuation marks

THE FULL STOP [.]

This is the strongest mark, making the most definite pause in reading aloud or silently. It is used at the end of sentences unless they are questions, strong exclamations or strong commands. It is also called a *period* and a *full point*.

It is used to indicate omitted letters in **abbreviations**, such as *a.m.* for *ante meridiem*, and in **initials**, as in *B. K. Smith*.

With a **contraction**, where the last letter of the contracted form is the last letter of the original word, no full stop is needed (e.g., *Dr* for *Doctor*).

Full stops are often used in amounts of money: £10.20 and in times: 3.20 a.m. When used as decimal points, they are usually typed as full stops but strictly should be raised above the line [·], as in 9·66.

Three full stops together (the **ellipsis** or suspension dots) [. . .] are used to show the omission of part of a sentence: *The letters of the alphabet are a, b, c . . . x, y, z*, or an unfinished sentence: *She would invite him to . . . No, that was unthinkable.*

THE QUESTION MARK [?]

This ends a direct question where an answer is expected: *'Where do I buy a ticket?'* It is not used for an indirect question (which reports a direct question), to which no answer is expected: *She asked where she could buy a ticket.* It is used at the end of rhetorical questions, where no answer is expected, e.g., *'Are you crazy?'* A question mark is needed when question phrases (question tags) are added to statements: *'The concert is tonight, isn't it?'*

THE EXCLAMATION MARK [!]

This is used after exclamations showing surprise: *'Fancy meeting you here!'* or strong emotion: *'You filthy cheat!'* or special emphasis: *'You are so beautiful!'* or an expletive: *'Damn!'* It is used after strong commands or requests, especially where the voice would be raised in speech: *'Don't shoot!'* Mild requests or commands usually end with a full stop: *'Come here, please.'* Using too many exclamation marks weakens their impact.

THE COMMA [,]

A **comma** has many uses, including:

1.   To separate items in a list:

Jake stole her purse, keys, cheque book and credit cards.

There is no need for a comma before the 'and' unless the sense demands it. The comma before the final 'and' is helpful in:

The children played cops and robbers, hide and seek, and hopscotch.

Some people use commas before *and* even in simple lists. This is called a serial comma, or Oxford comma, and is used as standard in the US.

2.   To separate two or more adjectives which individually modify a noun:

He was a small, shy, sickly, red-headed child.

There is no comma after the last adjective, and the commas carry the sense of *and*. If the last adjective and the noun form a single unit of meaning, there is no need for a comma before the final adjective as there is no sense of *and* connecting the two adjectives:

He was a great mathematical genius.

3.   In pairs, to separate descriptive phrases or clauses, or less important material, from the main part of the sentence:

Her sports car, painted a vivid orange, was parked illegally.

Omitting the first comma initially suggests that her car could paint; omitting the second comma initially suggests that a vivid orange was parked: both commas are needed, operating as a pair.

Where correct punctuation is used, the reader should not have to re-read a sentence to make sense of it. The test for the correctness of this use of a pair of commas is to read what precedes the first comma and what follows the second, omitting the words between the commas. The result should still make sense:

Her sports car was parked illegally.

It is most important to know the difference between phrases or clauses that merely **comment**, which have a pair of commas separating them off, and phrases or clauses that are **defining**, where a pair of commas would give the wrong meaning. In:

The boys, who were fit, enjoyed the race.

who were fit is commenting: this implies that all those boys were fit and all enjoyed the race. In:

The boys who were fit enjoyed the race.

who were fit is defining: only those boys who were fit enjoyed the race; those boys who were not fit did not enjoy it.

The presence or absence of a comma can change the meaning:

(i) *She liked Tony, who played cricket better than John.*

(ii) *She liked Tony, who played cricket, better than John.*

In (i), *better* refers to *played cricket*, but in (ii), *better* refers to *liked Tony*, as the words between commas are now a descriptive aside.

Note the effect of omitting the comma from these sentences:

(i) *She hoarded silver, paper and rags.*

(ii) *We ate chocolate, cakes and ices.*

4. To separate parts of compound or complex sentences, to aid comprehension by separating different ideas:

Although he was already deeply in debt, he bought her an expensive ring.

Do not, however, separate the subject from the verb, unless a commenting section comes between them. Wrong: *Such extravagant, distracting gestures, should not be used when speaking to a small audience.* The second comma is wrong as it hinders the flow of meaning from the subject, *gestures*, to the verb part, *should not be used.*

5. To separate sentence modifiers such as *moreover, indeed, however*:

(i) *The submarine, however, continued its attack.*

(ii) *Indeed, I have never felt better.*

6. To separate parts of dates and addresses, and in opening and closing letters:

28, The Terrace,
London, SW19 6PY

14 October 2010

Dear Peter,
Thank you for your invitation. The answer is 'Yes, please!'
Yours sincerely,
Jacob

The comma after 28 is standard practice but there is no grammatical reason for it.

Some or all of those commas in the address are now often omitted, with moving to a new line acting as a kind of punctuation. The British Post Office prefers no punctuation in addresses, the post town in capitals, and the postcode on a separate line.

7.   To separate the figures within a number into groups of three, from right-to-left if there is no decimal point, or from the decimal point, going to the left only: *13,109,896; 4,678·9857; 0·987654.* In some countries commas are used where we put a full stop, and vice versa, which can be very confusing. In France, for example, 3·1 is written 3,1 and a million as 1.000.000.

8.   To separate two independent clauses (which could usually be written as separate sentences) that are joined by a coordinating conjunction (*and, but, or, nor, so, yet, either . . . or*):

> *It is necessary to eat, but it is better to combine necessity with pleasure.*

9.   To prevent even temporary misreading:

> *If you want to shoot the farmer will lend you his gun.*

This would be clearer as:

> *If you want to shoot, the farmer will lend you his gun.*

The first version initially implies shooting the farmer.

10.   To show the omission of a word or words whose meaning is understood:

He can tolerate no noise; she, no silence.

As mentioned on page 70, a very common error ('run-on sentences', with only a 'comma splice') is to use only a comma, without a conjunction, to join main clauses which could stand as separate sentences, each having a subject and finite verb. Wrong: *We went to the races at Ascot, it was beautifully sunny, the horses sweated heavily.*

Such 'sentences', if linked, should be joined by a stronger link than just a comma; a semicolon, or a comma plus a linking conjunction, should be used. Use a colon if a second 'sentence' explains, expands or summarises the first.

THE SEMICOLON [;]

The **semicolon** is an important but under-used punctuation mark. There are several major uses:

1.   To separate items in a list, especially where some items are long or contain commas, or to avoid misunderstandings:

> *At the zoo we saw a brown bear, which was suckling two tiny cubs; a sleepy crocodile; two stick insects, each looking like a dead twig; and five elephants.*

Having a semicolon, not a comma, after *cubs* avoids any implication that the bear was suckling all the other creatures. A comma is usually sufficient before the last item, but a semicolon here makes clear that the stick insects did not look like five elephants as well as like dead twigs.

2.   To separate clauses which could have been two different sentences but which are closely related in meaning and of similar importance:

> *It was long past midnight, in a remote part of the forest; she shivered with fear.*

Although one could use a full stop after *forest*, joining the sentences with a semicolon shows better that her action was related to the time and place.

Two statements joined by a semicolon may provide contrasting ideas:

> *The young often wish to be older; the old would prefer to be younger.*

The second or later statement may complement the first:

The road to Bristol seemed unusually smooth; the recent repairs had been costly but effective.

A colon could be used here instead of a semicolon.

3.   To come before linking words such as *therefore*, *nevertheless*, *however*, *besides*, when they join two independent clauses or sentences:

She hated London; nevertheless, she flourished there.

A semicolon is often equivalent to, and replaceable by, a comma plus a coordinating conjunction:

She liked Robert; he disliked her.

She liked Robert, but he disliked her.

With this equivalence, some textbooks state that it is wrong to have a semicolon followed by a coordinating conjunction (e.g., *and*, *but*, *for*, *nor*), but other books permit it.

Unless separating items in a list, semicolons are normally followed by a complete clause, with a subject and finite verb.

THE COLON [:]

A colon is generally a punctuation mark of introduction, signalling 'look ahead', rather than of separating or stopping things. It is used:

1.   To introduce a list:

I suggest the following for promotion: Enid Brown, Peter Scott and John Reid.

Use a colon (without a dash), never a semicolon, to introduce lists.

2.   To introduce direct speech:

   He said: 'I don't give a damn.'

A comma could be used instead of the colon.

3.   To introduce an explanation, expansion or summary of the first part of a sentence:

   There were two problems: his small income and her taste for luxury.

Colons are used in proportions: *a 3:1 ratio*, in times: 10:25:45 (45 seconds past 10.25 a.m.), and in references: Matthew 4:27.

There are occasions when either a colon or a semicolon could be used to join two sentences, but choose a colon if the second one expands, explains or summarises the first one, with the colon signalling 'look ahead!':

At last he told us Peter's secret: the old tramp had been wealthy but had gambled his fortune away.

BRACKETS [( )]

Brackets are used in pairs, to separate supplementary, subsidiary or explanatory material from the main flow of a sentence:

   Visitors arriving for the conference in Glasgow on 2 January (a bank holiday in Scotland) should make their own arrangements for lunch.

The material inside brackets can be referred to as being 'in parenthesis'. In equations, there may be different types of bracket, ( ), { }, [ ], to show different hierarchies of terms. Brackets are also used to enclose references, interruptions and afterthoughts:

> *Mr Brown's comments (letter, The Times, 3 Aug.) show a total ignorance of Germany's history.*

Brackets make a firmer separation of the enclosed material than do two commas. If the words in brackets come at the end of a sentence, a full stop (or [?] or [!]) comes after the second bracket. If the words inside the brackets make a complete sentence, put a full stop (or [?] or [!]) before the closing bracket.

Square brackets, [ ], are used to enclose editorial comments or explanations in material written by a different author:

> *Rachael [his second wife] left the cottage to her sister Rebecca.*

THE DASH [– OR —]

A single **dash** is used:

1.   To mark a pause for effect:

> *She wore her most stunning dress – a billowing ocean of multi-coloured taffeta.*

2.   To introduce an afterthought, a summary, an elaboration or a change in direction of thought:

> *'I was in the artillery during the war – but I mustn't bore you with ancient history.'*

Pairs of dashes are used to show an interruption in the flow of thought, to enclose a side comment or a subsidiary idea:

> *His grandmother – a brilliant actress in her day – encouraged him to apply for the leading part.*

Pairs of dashes, brackets and commas are sometimes interchangeable, but may give a different emphasis.

Some writers and printers do not put **spaces before and after a dash**, but putting those spaces, as in the examples in points 1 and 2 in this section, helps to distinguish a dash from a hyphen. Distinctions are made between **en-dashes** (en-rules), originally the length of the letter 'n', and **em-dashes**, originally the length of an 'm'. En-dashes [–], without spaces, are used for a span, as in *The 1939–45 war*, or in joining names, as in *The Rome–Berlin axis*. En-dashes [–] or em-dashes [—], with or without spaces, are used to enclose commenting statements, as in: *His taste in clothes – which was appalling – had many followers*. The em-rule closed up is used in written dialogue to indicate an interruption, as in: *'Stop him from—', but it was too late.*

Some **word-processors** automatically put en-dashes and em-dashes where appropriate, but not always correctly. With most computers, en-dashes can be obtained by having the Num Lock on, holding Alt, and typing 0150, with 0151 for em-dashes. For most purposes, typing [hyphen/dash] is sufficient for an en-dash. In MS Word, the en-dash will automatically appear if the word following the dash is followed by a space.

THE HYPHEN [-]

The **hyphen** has no surrounding spaces and is a joining mark within words and compound expressions:

short-sighted, blue-eyed; do-it-yourself, non-stick.

American usage is often to omit the hyphen and that trend is apparent in British English, although '*blueeyed*' would be absurd. A hyphen is particularly useful to distinguish words with the same spellings but different meanings:

> To **re-cover** *the chair with velvet; to* **recover** *the chair from the rubbish dump.*

> To **resign** *from one's job; to* **re-sign** *the lease agreement.*

Hyphens are valuable for avoiding ambiguity. Note the difference between

> An *old-furniture seller* and An *old furniture-seller*.

Contrast *a cross-party group* of MPs with *a cross party group of MPs!*

An important and often neglected function of the hyphen is **to form compound adjectives.** These are made up of more than one word and should usually be hyphenated if they apply only jointly, not separately, to the noun. In *fund-raising activities, fund-raising* is a compound adjective, with *fund* and *raising* not applying separately to *activities*.

If the first word is an adverb, hyphens are not usually needed: *a very pretty woman.* Hyphens are used with adverbs if necessary to avoid ambiguity, as in *a little-known actor;* that hyphen shows that *little* is an adverb qualifying *known*, not an adjective referring to his height.

A common fault is to use **the prefix *non*** as if it were a separate word. There is no such word as *non* in normal English, so *non aggression treaty* is wrong; the *non* must be hyphenated to the following word: *non-aggression.* A *non-profit-making organisation*

needs both hyphens because it would be a non organisation,
a profit organisation and a making organisation, if each word
applied separately.

Sometimes it is optional whether one hyphenates words,
leaves them separate, or combines them, e.g., water-bed,
water bed, waterbed. *Non-aggression treaty* and *nonaggression
treaty* are both acceptable, unlike *nonprofitmaking*.

A phrase forming a compound adjective before a noun may need
hyphens, as in *an out-of-breath runner*, without needing them
elsewhere, as in *The runner was out of breath.*

A hyphen is often used if combining two words, or a prefix
or a suffix with a main word, would result in two identical vowels
or three identical consonants coming together from different
component parts of the word: *pre-emptive; co-own; grass-seed. Contraaction* is better than *contraaction* (which looks like a misspelling of
contraction); *anti-incendiary* is better than *antiincendiary*.

Hyphens are used when writing fractions used as adjectives:
*By the age of twenty, he had spent his one-third share of his father's
legacy. One third of the class* would not have a hyphen after *one*, as
one third is then a noun phrase, not adjectival.

The hyphen is used to **divide a word at the end of a line**.
Do not divide one-syllable words and do not divide a word so as
to leave only one letter before or after the division. In general,
divide words at the ends of syllables (pronounce them, if unsure
where the syllables end, e.g., mi-cro-scop-ic). Avoid distracting
fragments such as *the-rapist, depart-mental.*

THE APOSTROPHE [']

This has several uses:

1. To indicate that letters have been omitted: *don't* (do not); *I'll* (I will or I shall); *it's* (it is or it has). **Do not use an apostrophe in possessive pronouns**: *its, hers, his, ours, yours, theirs,* but there is one in *one's.*

2. To form **plurals** of expressions or letters with no natural plural: *Dot your i's and cross your t's.* Here the combination *'is'* and *'ts'* might be confusing. One can use quotes rather than apostrophes: *'i's* and *'t's.*

3. To form the **possessive case** of a noun:

(i) With a singular noun, add an apostrophe and an *s* to the basic form: *John, John's hat; the car, the car's wheels.* One may **optionally** omit the 's' if it makes an awkward combination of *s*-sounds: *James's house* sounds fine but the 's' may be omitted from *James' serious suspicions; Moses' sandals* is easier to say than *Moses's sandals.*

If two owners of the same thing are named in the same sentence, put the apostrophe after the second name, not both:

We visited John and Anne's house,
not *We visited John's and Anne's house.*

(ii) With a plural noun, only add the apostrophe if the plural ends in *s* already: *the two boys' bicycles; the ladies' hats.*

(iii) If the plural noun does not end in *s*, add an apostrophe and an 's': *the men's choice; the people's reactions.*

Never use an apostrophe in the plurals of ordinary words which are not possessive. Wrong: *Cheap cauliflower's! Bargain shirt's.* These are ordinary plurals, with no sense of possession, whereas *The shirt's price* needs an apostrophe, showing possession of the price by the shirt. Such wrong apostrophes in plurals are often called 'greengrocers' apostrophes'.

The **power of the apostrophe** is shown with the headline: *Briton's battle fatigue.* This was an account of one Briton's battle fatigue. If the apostrophe had been after the '*s*', it would indicate the battle fatigue of more than one Briton. Without the apostrophe, *Britons battle fatigue*, the word *battle* changes from a noun to a verb, indicating that more than one Briton was battling with fatigue, not battle fatigue specifically.

QUOTATION MARKS [" "] OR [' ']

Quotation marks are also called inverted commas, speech marks or quotes. They are used in pairs to enclose direct speech; that is, the exact words spoken:

> *'We've won!' she shouted.*

Use common sense to decide where other punctuation comes in relation to them, but usages differ.

For direct speech, the closing quotation mark follows the full stop, question mark or exclamation mark at the end of the speech:

> *She asked, 'What is the weather like outside?'*
> *He said, 'It is raining.'*

For titles of plays or other non-spoken quotations, the quotation mark at their end comes before the sentence's final punctuation mark:

Last night we saw 'The Importance of Being Earnest'.

When a quotation comprises several sentences, the end quotation mark comes after completion of the last sentence:

He said, 'It has been a long day. You look exhausted. I suggest we go home.'

Some other languages use different quotation marks, e.g., « French » or „German".

When the words spoken come before the verb relating to the act of saying, they are followed by a comma (or [?] or [!]) before the closing inverted comma, not by a full stop, even though the spoken sentence has ended:

'I'm going to France soon,' she declared.

Where the spoken sentence is broken by the subject and verb of saying, the continued speech after the break is still the same spoken sentence and so continues with a small letter (unless the first word is a proper noun):

'It is my wish', the comedian said, 'to bring laughter to this troubled world.'

In quoted speech lasting more than one paragraph, there is an initial quotation mark and one at the beginning of each subsequent paragraph to indicate that the speech continues, but no quotation mark at the end of each paragraph (the speech has not finished), until the final closing quotation mark. In some novels, quotation marks are omitted from dialogue.

Although sets of either single or double inverted commas can be used – publishers have different conventions – using double inverted commas avoids possible confusion when an apostrophe follows a final 's'. For example, in: *are often called 'greengrocers' apostrophes'*, it is not immediately clear whether the marks after 'greengrocers' or 'apostrophes' are apostrophes or closing single quotation marks. It would be clearer to write: *are often called "greengrocers' apostrophes"*.

For quotations within quotations, one alternates single and double inverted commas:

> *The colonel said: 'My happiest times as a soldier were with "the boys in the bush" in Africa.'*

Inverted commas can be used to enclose slang, dialect or foreign expressions, and technical or other terms that seem out of context:

> (i) *He punched him in the 'bread basket'.* (slang for stomach)

> (ii) *Her natural 'joie de vivre'* (French for 'joy of living') *was accentuated by champagne.*

Italics without inverted commas are also used for this purpose.

Inverted commas are occasionally used to enclose the titles of books, plays, poems, newspapers, etc., but are often omitted. Italics are now often preferred to quotation marks for titles, slang and foreign expressions.

Inverted commas are used when words are employed in a sarcastic, ironic or figurative sense:

> *She is our 'Margaret Thatcher'.* [The strong lady of our group]

I don't know what girls see in him; it must be his 'good looks'.
[He is ugly]

THE SLASH [/]

The **slash** is also known as the solidus, slant, oblique, oblique stroke or simply the stroke. It is used in fractions: *3/5ths of the distance*; in dates: *21/12/02*; to show alternatives: *Your coach/train/ boat ticket; He/she should go* . . . Both the forward slash (/) and the backslash (\ ) are used in computing.

THE CARET [λ], [∧] OR [^]

The caret (pronounced 'carray') indicates where omitted material (usually shown above in smaller print) is to be inserted. The above symbols do not display correctly on all systems. The first is an upside-down letter *y*; the second is an upside-down letter *v*; the third resembles the French and Portuguese circumflex but serves a different purpose.

Other punctuation or typographical devices

THE CAPITAL LETTER

Capital (upper-case) letters are visual symbols, helping the reader in the same way as punctuation marks. They are used at the beginning of a sentence or piece of speech; in proper names (*Janet Smith, Senate House*); in titles, for example, of people, plays, films, books and newspapers (*the Prime Minister, The Tempest, The Spy Who Loved Me, the Daily Mail*); in days of the week; in months; in the name of *God*, and in the pronoun *I*.

Capitals are not used for the seasons (*spring, winter*), nor for points of the compass unless part of a proper name: 'Go *east*, to *East Sheen*.' In titles, less important words such as *a, of,* or *the,* often do not have a capital letter, as in *The Applied Genetics of Humans, Animals, Plants and Fungi*.

Do not use a capital letter for a word which had a capital as part of a title, but is no longer part of a title: *This morning Prince Charles opened the bridge over the River Crane. He then sailed up the river in a yacht.* In the second sentence, *river* is not part of a title.

The importance of using the right case, upper or lower, is shown by the differences between a *DSC* (a military award, the Distinguished Service Cross) and a *DSc* (an academic higher doctorate, Doctor of Science), a *ford* (crossing point over a stream) and a *Ford* (car), and a *fiat* (decree) and a *Fiat* (car).

A distinction is made overtly when people say things such as: '*I'm a conservative with a small "c".*' That means that they are conservative in views but not associated with the Conservative Party.

If you use a **German noun** as an unassimilated foreign word, it must have an initial capital letter wherever it occurs in the sentence, as in *The cruel man's* Schadenfreude *was excessive*.

In scientific Latin names, by international convention, the genus always has a capital letter and the species always has a small (lower-case) letter, even if based on a proper name: *Salmonella typhimurium*; *Rosa chinensis*; *Homo sapiens*. Newspapers frequently get such capitals and lower-case letters wrong. In English, adjectives of nationality have a capital letter: *a New Zealand wine*; *Australian humour*. Adjectives derived from proper names have a capital letter: *Mendelian laws* (from Mendel).

ITALICS

Italics or cursive script, with sloping print, are used to show special emphasis, as in:

'You were meant to come *next* Tuesday, not today!'

When spoken, the part in italics would be said emphatically. Italics are used for the titles of books, newspapers, films and similar items. Scientific names are usually printed in italics: *Homo sapiens*. Latin and other foreign words used in English are often printed in italics, such as *in situ* [in place] and *bon mot* [clever remark]. In *a priori* [from first principles], having the *a* in italics helps prevent one initially misreading it as the indefinite article, a. As in this book, italics can be used to highlight examples, to make them stand out from descriptive text.

BOLD TYPE

Bold-face type is heavier than ordinary type. It is used to make certain words stand out from the rest, as in headword entries in a dictionary, to distinguish them from definitions. It is often used for section headings.

UNDERLINING

Underlining or **underscoring** was used on old-fashioned typewriters for emphasis or Latin names. It has largely been replaced by bold type or italics, respectively. Underscored spaces are sometimes used in computing, especially in e-mail addresses, such as john_smith@xyz.com, where there is an underscored space between *john* and *smith*, although underlining of the whole expression may obscure it. A wartime poster used underlining for emphasis, capital letters for clarity and impact, and moving to a new line as a kind of punctuation – but not consistently:

> <u>YOUR</u> COURAGE
> <u>YOUR</u> CHEERFULNESS
> <u>YOUR</u> RESOLUTION
> WILL BRING
> US VICTORY

THE SPACE

The **space** is not normally listed as a punctuation device but it is the commonest of all and is vital to show where one word ends and another begins. Many of the earliest manuscripts had no spaces between the words, making them hard to read:

Althoughonecanwithdifficultymakeoutwhatmighthavebeen intendedhavingspacesandotherpunctuationmakescomprehension mucheasier.

Note the difference between *The rapists are evil* and *Therapists are evil; Her cake was not iced* and *Her cake was noticed*. A space can change a specific type, such as a *blackbird*, into a general type, such as a *black bird*, which includes crows and rooks.

BULLET POINTS

Bullet points can be various shapes, including circles, diamonds, ticks, arrows or a pointing hand. They may be used for:

- lists
- a series of related points
- display purposes.

Punctuation at the end of each item should be consistent but users' practices vary. Some people use no punctuation at the end of each item, or a full stop after the last item only, or semicolons after each item, or full stops after each item.

COMPUTERS AND CHARACTER SETS

Early **computers** used a limited set of characters, while later models provided fuller sets including foreign letters, accented letters and currency symbols, e.g., ß, é, ¥. There have been different systems at different times, and the extra characters on one computer may come out differently on other computers or printers.

The following marks are part of the original ASCII character set and should transfer correctly: full stop, colon, semicolon, question mark, exclamation mark, hyphen, slash, brackets (round, square, curly), vertical single and double quotes (the same for opening and closing quotations). Problems may arise with: 'curly quotes', single and double (where opening and closing quotes differ), en-dash, em-dash, ellipsis, caret, raised decimal point, currency symbols, accented and foreign letters.

When using Microsoft Windows, extended character sets can be found using Start > All Programs > Accessories > System Tools > Character Map, then choosing the font and scrolling down to the desired character. This can be copied [Ctrl C] and pasted [Ctrl V] or one can record the key combination to use with the Num Lock on; for example, Alt+0183 for a raised decimal point [·], Alt+094 for a caret [^]. For foreign accents, see pages 201–2.

CHAPTER 13

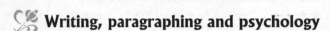

Writing, revising and readers' psychology

Writing, paragraphing and psychology

INTRODUCTION

How you should write depends on the importance, nature and length of the document, and on how much time you have. A job application, a CV, a work for publication, or examined theses or essays deserve much more attention than a casual note to an old friend.

For many pieces of writing, you need to consider most of the following points:

- What is its purpose, its desired effect?
- Who are the intended readers and how much background knowledge do they have?
- What length, form and style are appropriate?
- Should there be any subdivisions, perhaps by subheadings?
- Are any displayed items needed, such as tables, graphs, illustrations or photos?
- Are the 'facts' really true?
- Should the piece have an attention-grabbing title?

Your readers may be busy (or lazy) people and have lots of rival things to do besides reading what you have written, so you should think about their needs and preferences. Try to **start with a strong sentence** to catch each reader's interest, then aim for a logical flow of information, right through to the conclusion of the piece.

Unless the item is short, simple or routine, **jot down the main points** to include. **Decide on the best order** for presenting them, with one topic leading naturally to another.

PARAGRAPHING AND THE PSYCHOLOGY OF READERS

The **first paragraph** should set out what you are trying to do. If possible, start each paragraph with a sentence introducing its subject matter; develop that subject within the paragraph, then provide a link with the next paragraph.

Paragraph length is surprisingly important in the perceived readability of a work. Paragraphs of half a page or more have a deterrent effect on many readers, making them think that reading is going to be difficult, whether it is or not. Popular newspapers often use very short paragraphs, frequently of one or two sentences. In the action sections of novels, sentences and paragraphs tend to be short.

Your readers' psychology needs to be considered: they are only human! For a reader, getting to the end of a paragraph represents welcome progress, just as getting to the end of a chapter can. This has been exploited almost to the limit by James Patterson in his fast-moving thrillers. His book, *I, Alex Cross*, has 117 chapters in 374 pages! The book's US publisher commented that *An ancillary benefit of the short chapters is that for people who find reading challenging, there's a sense of accomplishment.*

If a paragraph looks too long to you as author, it will to the reader, so see if there is a suitable point to divide it. Try to avoid paragraphs of only one sentence, although they are not wrong.

When we are enjoined to save paper, it might seem odd to advocate increasing the amount of white space in a document, but **readers like white space** and **visual variety**. Large blocks of uninterrupted text can look daunting. White space is space not occupied by print. Leaving generous margins round each page may increase acceptability.

The set of **bullet points** near this chapter's beginning conveys sentences well separated by space, and easier to follow than if written as continuous text. With computers, one can adjust **font size** to improve legibility, as well as the **spacing** between lines and between paragraphs. There should be a line of space after headings, but no punctuation at the end of headings or subheadings unless they pose questions.

If the piece is long, with contrasting sections, **subheadings** can help the writer and the reader. You may need subheadings within subheadings, as in this chapter; you can use **bold print** or CAPITAL LETTERS to distinguish different levels of heading.

People like **visual effects**, such as illustrations, cartoons, photos, diagrams or graphs. They can enhance and clarify the text, although there is a danger that they may distract attention from your words.

FURTHER ADVICE

Check your facts and figures. It infuriates me to see a bacterium described as a virus or vice versa. One article dealt with a canker disease damaging conker trees and referred to *'a new bacteria'* (that should be *a bacterium*) which is *'part of a large genus of fungal pathogens'*. A bacterium is not a fungus. One obvious error makes a reader doubt the accuracy of the whole piece.

Try to offer **variety in sentence structure and length**, with a mixture of simple, complex and compound sentences (pages 65–8). Consider whether the **active or passive voice** (pages 52–3) is more appropriate in particular contexts.

Use correct grammar, spelling and punctuation – and the Queen's English.

Do not rely on **computer spell-checkers and grammar-checkers**. They will not pick up *casual* for *causal*, or *affect* for *effect*. They will pick up typing errors which produce non-existent words such as *casal*, but you have to choose the correct alternative from the suggested list, e.g., *canal, casual, causal*. They may also pick up wrong parts of speech.

Check whether your use of **tenses** (pages 50–2) is correct and consistent. If you use **figures of speech** (pages 140–3), are they appropriate or are they dull clichés? In formal writing, avoid slang and contractions.

If you use **foreign expressions**, check for agreements in number and gender, e.g., *femmes fatales*, *fiancé* (male), *fiancée* (female).

Check for **consistency in points of view**. For example, if giving instructions do not change between *one should*, *you should* and *we should* unless there is a good reason for switching.

If there are **tables** or **illustrations**, find suitable places in the text for them, or put them at the end. They are most useful when seen at the same time as the text referring to them.

When you reach the end of your piece, a short **summary paragraph** may be appropriate, but avoid undue repetition. Have you overstated or understated your case, hedged excessively, or failed to give a firm decision if one is required? If you have written **dialogue,** is it clear to the reader who is speaking at any time?

✄ Revising your work

Leave time to revise your piece. It is easy to miss out important words such as *not*. The publishers of the 'Wicked Bible' in 1631 were heavily fined for inadvertently omitting the word *not* from the Seventh Commandment (Exodus 20:14): 'Thou shalt commit adultery.'

You might use the wrong word, write incomplete sentences, miss out facts or ideas, and make many kinds of error, especially when writing under time pressure. Revising your work could save time in the long run, compared with sending a faulty missive and trying to undo its harm later.

Good writers check thoroughly. Check everything, including the sense and the impression given. Check any computer-produced underlinings for spelling or grammatical errors. Check sentence and paragraph structure and length.

Your **first draft** enables you to put everything together, to see the piece as a whole. Your revision of it can improve effectiveness and clarity, as well as eliminating errors. Check for weak sentences which add little and for possible confusions over pronouns. See also the advice on business writing (pages 184–97).

Revise for **clarity, correctness, consistency, conciseness** and **completeness**. If your piece is in response to another one, have you answered all necessary points? Do shorten the first draft. You can often shorten a piece by about one quarter and simultaneously improve its clarity and information flow. Are there any unneeded words or opinions; or is there any redundant information you can delete? Woolliness, excessive wordiness and length may alienate readers and cause them to give up. Have you spelled out any unusual **acronyms** at their first use?

For an important document, get friends or colleagues to check it as they often spot flaws which the author has missed. If you can leave an appreciable time between your own re-readings, that helps you to see things with fresh eyes.

 Publication

If writing for publication, make sure that you follow that publisher's **guide for authors**, and that your target publisher does accept your kind of item. The *Writers' & Artists' Yearbook* can be very useful. Many rapid-publication journals such as *Nature* require electronic **camera-ready copy**, so that you do all the layout. You must follow the instructions exactly on page size, spacings, font type and size for different types of text and headings, illustrations, how to quote references, etc. If American spelling is specified, use it. Most publishers require an electronic copy of your work as well as printed copies of double-spaced text.

Check each set of proofs very carefully. It is amazing **what can go wrong** even when the publisher does not need to have the work retyped. If a change is made by you or the editor, check whether it necessitates further changes elsewhere.

CHAPTER 14

Writing formal letters

When writing informally to friends, you will probably follow whatever style is common in your group. When writing **formal letters**, however, there are conventions to respect.

Start with your full address, including the postcode and telephone number(s). If relevant, add your e-mail address. Then give the name and address of the addressee, although you could omit those if you know the person well. Always give the **date**. If replying to a communication which has a date or a **reference number**, quote it or them.

Address the letter to *Dear*, then give the title and name of the addressee, such as *Miss Williams*, *Professor Roberts* or *Major Plumbe*. There are published lists of formal terms of address, for example, when addressing the Queen or an archbishop, but most people will not need them.

Women's titles, if unknown, present a problem. Some women prefer *Miss* or *Mrs*, as appropriate, and hate that politically correct Americanism *Ms*; others prefer *Ms*. If you know the woman's forename, you could omit the unknown title and write, for example, to *Ruth James*.

Make an effort to get the addressee's name correct as people feel strongly about their names. Distinguish between Elizabeth/Elisabeth, Lesley/Leslie, Isobel/Isabelle, Ann/Anne, Thompson/Thomson, Johnstone/Johnson, for example.

Using proper grammar, spelling and punctuation, write the **main text** of your letter politely and concisely, with a logical sequence of material. Try to get a connected flow between sentences and paragraphs.

As an **ending**, *Yours sincerely* is used when the recipient's name is known, and *Yours faithfully* when it is not. *Yours truly* is more old-fashioned but may be used when the writer wishes to meet the recipient. *With best wishes* (or *Best wishes*) is common and acceptable. Your signature, preferably legible, should follow. Underneath that, print your name and, if relevant, your status and qualifications.

Check that the envelope is correctly addressed and stamped, and that any necessary enclosures are included.

Here is a specimen short business letter, polite but to the point. See also Business Writing, pages 184–97.

Stone Cutters of Richmond
94 London Road
West Richmond
TW16 7RR
020 8946 3332
j.evans@stonecutters.co.uk

Mr R. Oliver
Sales Department
Grinding Gears
28 Taggart Road
Ipswich IP6 6PR

28th January 2010

Your reference E1967

Dear Mr Oliver,

Thank you for your estimate, dated 14/1/2010, for a new gearbox
for our cutting machine, Butler Swiftcut, model 683. Your price
is too high and there are alternative suppliers. Could you make
some reduction, or include transport to our factory in the cost?

Yours sincerely,
[signature]
John Evans, BSc (Eng)
Factory Manager

CHAPTER 15

Are you ambiguous?

Introduction

Ambiguity occurs when something can be understood in more than one way, possibly causing confusion or the wrong message being understood. The many **causes of ambiguity** include unclear handwriting, ambiguity of individual words, and grammatical problems such as wrong pronoun relations, word-order problems and misplaced modifiers.

Some potential causes of ambiguity, such as the use of the abbreviation *m* for millions, miles and metres, are often resolved by **common sense** and **context**: *I came third in the 10,000 m race* is not ambiguous if it refers to running.

Hanging participles were dealt with on page 57. For example, in *Riding my bicycle, the dog kept up a good pace*, the implication is that the dog was riding my bicycle.

Word and name ambiguity

Is this statement ambiguous?

This showed that the lab air was quite pure.

The problem is that **quite** has different meanings. In *She was quite dead*, *quite* means *completely, totally*. In *She was quite pretty*, *quite* means *somewhat, partly*, not totally. Did the experiment show that the lab air was somewhat pure, or that it was totally pure? We cannot tell.

The word **right** can mean *correct* or *in a right-hand direction*. A car approaches an important junction:

> *Driver: 'Do I turn left at the traffic lights?'*
>
> *Passenger with map: 'Right.'*
>
> *The driver, thinking that the passenger means turn right, turns right.*
>
> *Passenger: 'You idiot! I agreed with you about turning left.'*

Ambiguities can usually be resolved by rewording or hyphenating.

> *Forty odd people were present.*

This could be put as *About forty people were present*, or *Forty-odd people were present* or, less likely, *Forty peculiar people were present*.

There are many **geographical ambiguities** with the names of streets, villages, towns, cities and rivers, with more than ten towns called *Newcastle* in different countries, several rivers called *Avon* in Britain, and so on. There are many ambiguities with **names of people and firms**. There are so many people with common names that it pays to be very specific, e.g., asking a firm's switchboard for the John Smith who works in sales of machinery to Australia.

Be careful about deducing gender from names. **Sexually ambiguous names** include *Robin*, *Valerie*, *Hilary*, and shortened names such as *Sam*, *Jo* and *Alex*. In Britain, *Samantha* is normally female, but in Sri Lanka a hotel manager called *Samantha* was a heavily bearded man!

Pages 167–75 have examples of words which are often confused, sometimes causing ambiguity. **Homographs** (words with different meanings but spelled the same, pages 179–80) cause problems in written English, while **homophones** (words which sound alike, page 181) cause ambiguity in spoken English. This is exploited in jokes such as:

'Is life worth living?'

'It all depends on the liver!'

There are ambiguities from a careless choice of words. An A-level biology student wrote:

A poplar tree can break wind at a distance of up to 200 metres.

Presumably *act as a wind break* was intended, not *fart*.

Word-order ambiguity

Here there is ambiguity:

I saw two huge lobsters scuba-diving in the wreck.

That would be clearer as:

When I was scuba-diving, I saw two huge lobsters in the wreck.

In the following sentence, were the clams fed to the professor or the starfish?

Professor Thomas examined autoradiographs of starfish digestive tissue after being fed radioactive clams.

If **modifying words**, phrases or clauses are too far from the words they modify, then ambiguity or absurdity can arise:

Algernon was trampled by an elephant wearing only his pyjamas.

This would be much better as *Algernon, wearing only his pyjamas, was trampled by an elephant.*

Karen still goes to the pub where she had her arm broken regularly.

The adverb *regularly* would be better placed after the verb to which it refers, *goes*, not after *had . . . broken*.

Adjectives and ambiguity

On page 85, we saw that ambiguity may occur when an adjective could apply to more than one following noun:

I ate the large duck's egg. Which was large, the duck, the egg or both?

135

We admired the ancient history teacher.

One can recast that sentence to remove the ambiguity:

We admired the teacher of ancient history or *We admired the ancient teacher of history.*

One could use hyphens: *an ancient-history teacher* or *an ancient history-teacher.*

Adjectives may or may not carry over to subsequent nouns, causing ambiguity. Suppose a label states:

These chocolates contain no artificial flavourings or preservatives.

Does that mean 'no preservatives' (eat quickly!), or 'no artificial preservatives'? We cannot tell.

Hyphens are wonderful for avoiding ambiguity:

To recount a story. To re-count the votes.

Four year-old sheep. Four-year-old sheep.

In *extra marital sex, extra* means *additional*; in *extra-marital sex, extra* means *outside the marriage.*

🌹 Ambiguities from different usages

We find **ambiguities from different national usages**. In the USA, *corn* means maize; in Britain, *corn* usually means *wheat* unless one specifies *sweet corn*, which is maize. *Pants* usually means *underpants* in Britain but *trousers* in the USA. A visiting American academic asked me what colour pants he should wear for cricket. I told him that the colour of his pants didn't matter but he should wear white trousers. A dangerous confusion comes from *pavement*, which in the UK means the path for walking beside a road, but in the USA means the road surface for vehicles.

There have been problems with foreign doctors working in the UK not understanding **colloquialisms** used here, such as *having a bun in the oven* (being pregnant) or *spending a penny* (using the toilet).

Ambiguity from pronouns

Ambiguity can arise if we cannot tell to which noun a pronoun applies. In *Joan told Mary that she was pregnant*, who was pregnant?

Ambiguities in comparisons

Consider: *My house is twice as big as yours*.

Does that refer to height, width, floor area, volume or number of rooms?

Handwriting, computers, printers and text messages

In my **handwriting**, it is not always easy to tell apart the words *wine*, *urine* and *wire*, although usually the context makes it clear which word is intended. If there is an important word where my handwriting may be unclear, I write it in capital letters, in square brackets, after the lower-case version. Check a sample of your handwriting for possible ambiguities, then get someone else to check it too.

Often **it is crucial** to get a particular letter right. Adults who cannot digest the milk sugar *lactose* have ceased to produce the digestive enzyme *lactase*, so bacteria in the lower intestines make large and embarrassing amounts of gas. It is essential to distinguish between *lactose* and *lactase*, in handwriting and print, as in other cases of *-ose/-ase* endings.

Some **computers, screens** and **printers** fail to distinguish between numeral *1*, capital letter *I*, as in *India*, and lower-case *l*, as in *lower*. Mine does not clearly distinguish capital *I* from lower-case *l*, which could cause problems if I were printing some security code such as *61lPlZI59*. The symbol after the 'P' is only marginally different from the one after the 'Z' with my computer, screen and printer.

In **text messaging**, there is no standardisation of abbreviations, which can cause ambiguities. For example, some people use *LoL* or *lol* for *lots of love*, while others use it for *laughing out loud*.

CHAPTER 16

Idioms, figures of speech, clichés and popular phrases

Introduction

Idioms, figures of speech, clichés and popular phrases often overlap. At school many of us were taught traditional comparisons such as *dry as a bone*, or *hard as nails*. Those are **figures of speech** called **similes**; they are also **clichés** because they are overused, like many **popular phrases**. Avoid such tired phrases, although they tend to spring readily to mind.

Figures of speech can add vividness and life to prose. They are widely used in **poetic imagery**, as in Robert Burns's 'A Red, Red Rose':

> O, my Luve's like a red, red rose . . .

Idioms

In **idioms**, the words taken together have a different meaning from their separate literal meanings, as in *It was raining cats and dogs*, where it was raining but with no animals falling from the sky, or *to spill the beans*, meaning to reveal the secrets, not to drop legumes, or *kick the bucket* (die).

You should use only idioms which your readers will understand. Patients using popular idioms, such as *I've got the trots* (diarrhoea), or *I'm dying for a leak* (urination), have sometimes confused doctors from overseas.

Figures of speech

METAPHOR

In **metaphors**, a descriptive word or phrase is applied to an object, person or action in an imaginative but not literal way, implying a resemblance without using words of comparison such as *like*. Thus Mrs Thatcher, a powerful and determined leader, was called *The Iron Lady. He soon found his feet* means that he became familiar with his surroundings, not that he discovered his lower limbs.

A common fault is to mix different metaphors or to continue without ending the metaphor. A headmaster wrote in a girl's end-of-year report:

> *Fiona has now found her feet which I hope will continue to success at GCSE.*

Mixed metaphors include:

> *In a nutshell, when he laid his cards on the table I smelled a rat, but I managed to nip it in the bud and so now the world's my oyster.*

SIMILE

In **similes**, a direct comparison is made, introduced by words such as *like, as, as if, as though*. Examples include:

*The nervous candidate shook **like a leaf**.*

*He was **as proud as a peacock**.*

HYPERBOLE

Hyperbole involves extreme exaggeration:

The teacher said to the dim pupil, 'I've told you a million times what hyperbole means!'

'I'd run a hundred miles to avoid his stinking breath,' she told her girlfriend.

METONYMY

In **metonymy,** one substitutes a part or an attribute for the whole thing, such as referring in a news item to *London* and *Beijing,* meaning the governments of *Britain* and *China,* or using *the turf* to mean *horseracing,* as in *He lost a small fortune on the turf.*

He watched the scanty bikini walk to the edge of the pool and dive in.

Here the bikini's actions were those of the woman wearing it.

ELLIPSIS

Ellipsis is the omission of words and is more common in poetry than prose. Compare the other use of ellipsis (plural, ellipses) to indicate omission using three spaced dots (page 99). In Shakespeare's *Macbeth* we see:

> *What! All my pretty chickens and their dam*
> *All at one fell swoop?*

The verb *taken* or *killed* is missing but easily understood. *Chickens and their dam* is a metaphor for his children and wife.

We can see ellipsis in prose: *He preferred beef; she, pork,* where the writer felt it unnecessary to repeat the verb.

EUPHEMISMS

Euphemisms are milder substitutions for words or phrases which might be considered rude or unpleasant. Death, sex, excretory functions and religion are the usual topics.

> *He passed away peacefully.* [passed away = died]

> *They slept together last night.* [slept together = had sexual intercourse]

> *Gordon relieved himself behind the tree.* [relieved himself = urinated]

In the account of a meeting, one might read: *A lively discussion ensued.* That could be a euphemism for *There was a blazing row.*

In *'It's bleedin' obvious, ain't it?'*, *bleedin'* is a euphemism for the swear word *bloody. Bloody* itself has been said to be a euphemism for the terms *By our Lady* or *Christ's Blood*, and was therefore regarded as very taboo in the nineteenth and early twentieth century. In Shaw's *Pygmalion* (1913), Eliza Doolittle's response: '*Walk! Not bloody likely*' caused a sensation, whereas today *bloody* is frequently used mindlessly as an intensifier.

The use of **swear words** in almost every sentence devalues their impact and suggests low intelligence in the swearer. While the Queen's English does encompass the use of swear words in extremely provoking circumstances, they should be kept to a minimum.

LITOTES

Litotes is a subtle device using the word *not*, usually followed by a word beginning with *un-*, in one of two different ways. The first is an **understatement** which is meant to be understood with much more force. *I was not a little underpaid* means that I was grossly underpaid.

The second use is for a **fine gradation** of meaning. In *The play was not unenjoyable*, the writer's view of the play falls between *was enjoyable* and *was not enjoyable*.

✁ Clichés

Clichés are expressions which have lost any liveliness through overuse. An apocryphal story has it that a journalist from a low-brow paper saw a Shakespeare play and criticised it for being absolutely full of clichés. In Shakespeare's time, however, the expressions were fresh, even if Shakespeare did not invent them all himself. In the late sixteenth century, these Shakespearean phrases must have sounded new:

Star-crossed lovers

To your heart's content

Hoist with your own petard

There's the rub

Gild the lily.

Today's clichés include: *cutting-edge research*; *at this moment in time*; *quantum leap*. When you check your work, eliminate them ruthlessly.

 Exercise (no answers are given)

- Write down two modern clichés which annoy you.

- Give two examples of common idioms.

- Devise examples of similes, metaphors, hyperbole, ellipsis, metonymy, litotes and euphemisms.

CHAPTER 17

Style and examples of excellent modern English

Style

Style is the manner in which a piece of writing or speaking is done. Your **choice of style** for a particular item depends on its recipients, your topic, your capabilities and your mood.

Handbooks often instruct a writer to choose **short, plain words** over longer, more elaborate ones, but rich language has its place. For instructions, agreements and forms, plainness and clarity are essential, but for creative or descriptive writing, vividness is often appropriate.

It is undesirable to repeat a word soon after its previous use. One can **avoid repetition** by using synonyms, near-synonyms or pronouns. Go for variety of words, sentence structure and length.

There are some very specialised styles, such as headlines in tabloid newspapers, where short words and no punctuation are preferred. Puns and even rhymes are used. Here are two classics from *The*

Sun, the first referring to the European Commission President in 1990, and the second to Samantha Cameron's 2010 pregnancy:

> *Up yours Delors*
>
> *Wham bam! Sam Cam to be mam (she'll need a new pram)*

By studying the following examples, you will get an idea of a range of styles. Consider how the writing differs in those styles, observing the choice of words, sentence structure and length, mood, and attitude to the subject matter and reader.

These examples are from finalists in the annual Queen's English Society's Arthur and Marjorie Goodchild Prize for Excellent English.

Lyrical country writing

Robin Page, *The Daily Telegraph, Weekend, 28/4/2007.*

This conjures up a vibrant picture.

> *The hour after dawn under an open sky is a beautiful time of birdsong, dewdrops and the lingering smell of scavenging foxes. As I walk over to the cows, with my exhaled breath white, to check for new arrivals, I leave a trail of wet footprints alongside those of badger, muntjac deer and fox. The foxes always turn up when there is the prospect of cow afterbirth to enjoy . . . They [sheep and cows on being let out in spring] ran, jumping and frisking, as they always do on release from their winter yard – heavily pregnant matrons with bellies bouncing and udders swinging are not one of nature's prettiest sights.*

The amusing sports report

Sue Mott, *The Daily Telegraph*, *Sport*, Wednesday, 29/6/2005.

This is a Wimbledon tennis commentary, with neat similes and metaphors.

> *Mary Pierce is what you might call a slow starter. For the first set of her quarter-final against the twice champion Venus Williams, she moved around the court like an underwater diving bell. Not that fast, actually. Michelangelo's David had more chance of returning Williams's first serve and the result was a very reflective 6–0 to the American in 21 locomotive minutes . . . Jolted awake, perhaps by shame, Pierce stopped performing as though stuck in a pool of aspic and fought all the way to an entrancing 22-point tie-break . . . It was an inexplicably statuesque performance from Pierce, with the emphasis on statue . . . It would be unfair to call 30-year-old Pierce a basket case. She is too elegant for that. She is more like a Prada handbag case . . .*

The polemic

Polemics should be truthful but extreme, not balanced.

Revd Dr Peter Mullen, *The Daily Telegraph*, 31/1/2008.

Although the piece makes entertaining reading, it is a deeply felt and courageous polemic against political correctness in the Church of England, and risks retribution from the Church authorities. The arguments are coherent and beautifully expressed, with many excellent turns of phrase.

I am trying to be a priest, but I haven't time. When I was first appointed vicar . . . the diocesan annual returns were on one side of A4 . . . Nowadays, the annual returns are a foot thick and a bundle of perfidious obscurity, hedged about with health and safety and absurd questions about light bulbs, and serious inquiries as to what the PCC is doing to reduce our carbon footprint – all because the Church has taken up the pagan fantasy of global warming. I think the returns are devised in some Kafkaesque archidiaconal madhouse and calculated to be impossible to complete even over the whole year.

. . . This is, of course, only political correctness tacked onto the failed collectivist socialist agenda that our rulers in the General Synod have foisted on us for a generation.

. . . It's a pantomime: a dumbed-down, clapped-out imitation of the entertainment industry combined with the newspeak of bureaucratic control. Once there was the Church of England. Now there is only the new Babel . . .

❧ The vivid description

Adam Nicolson, Commentary, *The Daily Telegraph*, 4/12/2004.

This bravura writing is full of startling imagery, of sounds, smells and action. The author describes three wrens *'living in a wren-shaped universe'*, so preoccupied with competing with each other that they completely ignore the huge number of much larger, noisier birds wheeling around them.

It was wren ballet, wren theatre, wren war . . . Wanderlust, intense mutual competition, aggressive territoriality, blindness to the existence of anything but themselves, all this combined with a male interest in engineering and female obsession with interior decor: it is an intriguingly human set of qualities.

The strangest sight I have seen all the year was during the summer, in an enormous seabird colony in the Hebrides. All round me, the puffins, razorbills and guillemots were hacking and growling at each other, standing in offended silence or simply coming and going, their babies cheeping deep within the boulders of the colony, the rocks coated in guanoed slime, the shags hissing and honking at me like demented witches, a stinking, ammonia-thick and frankly hellish place.

Spoofs and pastiches

A *spoof* is a parody, a mockery, while a *pastiche* is something in the style of a particular writer or period. This is a spoof recipe, not intended to be followed.

Oliver Pritchett, End column, *The Daily Telegraph,* 5/5/2004.

This rough, humorous piece is an excellent lampoon of recipe-speak and of chefs whose fame partly depends on their rudeness to gain publicity.

Break six eggs into a bowl and give them a good bollocking. Set aside. Now lay three lamb epithets on a board and pummel them for five minutes. By the end of this process, the lamb should be cowed, but not completely flattened. Take it outside and teach it a good lesson. Bring it back into the kitchen and sprinkle with asterisks, then pointedly ignore . . . Give the mixture a good glare and allow to vituperate . . . Excoriate a leek and denounce a medium-sized bulb of fennel, very roughly chopped, and stir-fry for two minutes.

✖ Broad dialect

Writing in dialect should only be attempted by those with a good ear for it. The piece should be generally understandable even if some words are obscure.

Gervase Phinn, *The Times*, *Life*, 8/6/2002.

Ten-year-old William, who speaks very broad Yorkshire, tells the author about his favourite tales from the Bible.

> 'Well, it's a cracking good tale, in't it? Old Goliath come-sa ovver dale, huffin' and puffin' and shoutin' and screamin' and wavin' his reight big sword abaat like there's no tomorra and tellin' t'Israelites to send out their champion. Out come little David wi' nowt but a slingshot in 'is 'and. "Waaay!" roars Goliath. "Is this t'best thy lot can do? Little squirt like thee! I could tread on thee and squash thee. I could breathe on thee and blow thee into t'next week."'

✖ The geographical description and travel writing

Note the use of dramatic language, the use of the active voice and nonstative (action) verbs (see pages 47, 52–3), and the excellent choice of adjectives.

Lynne Maxwell, published anonymously in *Practical Photography*, April 2004.

> Then head north to Upper Dovedale, where the ice must have hiccupped as it smoothed this plateau, leaving Chrome Hill and Parkhouse Hill rising from it like two 1,300 ft dorsal fins.

Now you're ready for the biggest, bleakest and best. The brooding plateau of Kinder Scout squats above Edale Moor, its top ironed flat by time and weather. At 2,087 ft it's the highest point in the Peak, and on a cold day you don't need confirmation of this from the contours on the map – your nose and toes will tell you. In the Peak District, lowland Britain rubs shoulders with the gritty uplands of the Pennines and you don't get much grittier than Kinder. Impossibly balanced rocky outcrops perch on its top with equally impossible shapes, sculpted smooth. And when mist cloaks the landscape, these dark tors and rocks become your guides, rising from the featureless waste to beckon you to safety.

Satire

Craig Brown, *The Daily Telegraph,* 11/11/2000.

This parody of the then Deputy Prime Minister's spoken English is in the best tradition of English satire, with inventive malapropisms, spoonerisms, 'Prescottisms' and tortured syntax. It starts:

> **7.15am:** *The alarm rock clings. Down to breakfast. Oil myself a beg, with hot tuttered boast.*

It ends with:

> *Tight first rhyme: the wrong kind of row on the snails.*

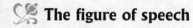 **The figure of speech**

Norman Lebrecht, *The Daily Telegraph*, 14/7/1999, 'on Music'.

> *It is not the custom of this column to speak ill of the dead, but the Arts Council of England has been giving so lively an impression of the proverbial headless chicken that some might be fooled into detecting signs of intelligent life.*

The obituary tribute

W. F. Deedes, *The Daily Telegraph*, 31/10/2003.

This tribute was given at Denis Thatcher's memorial service.

> *Denis Thatcher, whom we remember today, was the most straightforward and forthright of men, who'd deplore any false note struck in his memory . . . Denis left something imperishable. He left us the memory of a character, a stamp of man, straight and true, to which every father, whether soldier, man of business, sportsman or reptile might dearly wish their sons to aspire and if possible attain.*

CHAPTER 18

Ways to remember spellings and the use of word origins, prefixes and suffixes

Ways to remember spellings

Bad spelling gives an impression of carelessness and ignorance, and can lead to confusion and misunderstandings. It really helps to learn rules, to use a dictionary, and to use **word-origin clues**, **prefixes** and **suffixes**.

Learning a few rules will enable you to avoid **common blunders** such as *occured, assymetry, unaturally, definate, acheive, normaly, begining* and *dissapear*. Don't worry if some rules look complicated because the examples should make them clear. Even if you don't remember the rules, you can use the **pattern of a known word** to find the rule to apply. There are some exceptions, especially as *l, w* and *x* sometimes follow different rules.

Do try the exercises as they should help you remember the rules. Answers are not given but are in dictionaries.

USEFUL RULES

1. **Pronounce** the word carefully and use special 'mental pronunciations' to help remember words you find difficult. In your mind, you could pronounce and stress the second *n* of *environment*, or the *t* of *mortgage*.

2.   Pay attention to **long and short vowels** in your pronunciation. A short vowel often comes before a doubled consonant, especially if the consonant is not *l*, so use this when spelling *accommodation*. A long vowel followed by a consonant (not *w*, *x* or *y*) at the end of a word often indicates a silent final *e* after the consonant: *rob, robe; din, dine.*

3.   Keep a **record** of words you find difficult to spell. Write them out to help you learn the spelling, and devise a **mnemonic** (memory reminder) if possible.

4.   Use your **knowledge of related words** if troublesome unstressed vowels are not pronounced, or are pronounced unclearly. Different unstressed vowels may sound very similar, causing doubts about their spelling, as in the last vowel of *emigrant*. The *a* is a vague short sound which could be *er, a, e, u,* or *ur*. The very clear stressed *a* sound in the related word *emigration* helps you to guess the unstressed *a* in *emigrant*.

Exercise: Use this method to find the missing vowel [-] in: *defin-te, radi-nt, irrit-nt, environm-nt, degr-dation.*

5.   **Is it *ie* or *ei*?** The rule is: '**i before e except after c, if the vowel sound rhymes with bee.**' The last part of that rule is **most important** but people often omit it. This rule helps with *receive, achieve, believe, chief, receipt, deceive, brief,* etc. The few exceptions include *protein, caffeine* and *seize*. Where the vowel sound does **not rhyme with bee**, most words have *ei*: *deign, eider, feint, heifer, heir, reign, surfeit, vein, weigh,* but note *friend*.

6.   **Is it *c* or *s*?** By remembering *the advice* and *to advise*, where the noun *advice* (rhymes with *vice*) and the verb *advise* (rhymes with *lies*) are pronounced differently, you can work out other cases where the noun has *c* (*the practice, the licence*) and the verb has *s* (*to practise, to license*), even when the pronunciations do not differ.

7.   **Prefixes** are usually added to the base word without changes to either: *dis+solve = dissolve; dis+appear = disappear; mis+spell = misspell; inter+related = interrelated; inter+act = interact; un+natural = unnatural*. By knowing a **word's origin** from a prefix and a shorter word, one can work out the correct spellings, such as the double '*s*' in *dissolve* and the single '*s*' in *disappear*. The few exceptions usually involve '*l*': *all+together = altogether; well+come = welcome*.

8.   **Suffixes**
(a)   Suffixes beginning with a consonant ('consonant suffixes'), such as *ly*, do not usually change the base word: *normal+ly = normally; complete+ly = completely; govern+ment = government; hope+ful = hopeful*. The final '*e*' is sometimes dropped, as in *truly, duly, argument*.

(b)   Suffixes beginning with a vowel ('vowel suffixes'); *y* counts as a vowel here:

(i)   If the base word ends in a silent *e*, you generally drop that *e*: *hope, hoping; complete, completion*. The silent *e* is retained with a final *g* or *c* to keep the pronunciation of that consonant soft before suffixes beginning with *a* or *o*, as those vowels – unlike *e* and *i* – do not soften those consonants: *notice, noticeable* (*noticable* would be pronounced *notickable*); *outrage, outrageous*. The final *e* may be retained to prevent confusions: *dye, dyeing; die, dying*.

Exercise: Try these rules on *peace+able; forgive+ing; manage+able; manage+ing; stone+y; code+ing*.

(ii)   In words with one syllable and a single final consonant after a single vowel, you double the consonant when adding the vowel suffix: *hop, hopped; slim, slimmer; plan, planning* (without knowing such rules, one might put *hoped* or *planing*, changing the meanings).

(iii)   In words of one syllable ending with two consonants, or with two vowels together before a final consonant, you do not double the final consonant: *harp, harping; cool, cooling*.

(iv)   In words of two or more syllables ending in a single consonant preceded by a short vowel, you do not double the final consonant if the stress (shown by [']) is on the first syllable: *al'-ter, al'-tered; of'-fer, of'-fering*; if the stress is on the final syllable, you double the final consonant: *be-gin', be-gin'-ning; sub-mit', sub-mit'-ted; re-fer', re-ferred'*.

If adding the suffix changes the stress pattern, go by the stress pattern in the final word rather than in the base word: *re-fer'*, but *ref'-er-ence*, with a single *r* before the suffix because of the shift in stress. In words ending in *l* preceded by a short vowel, whether stressed or not, the *l* is usually doubled in Britain (but not in American English): *tra'-vel, travelled; com-pel', compelled*.

Exercise: Try this useful rule (iv), adding *-ed* to: *disbud, occur, differ, transmit, target, order, prefer, propel, commit, label*. Pronounce the words slowly if you are unsure which syllables are stressed, or stress each syllable in turn to find which version sounds right.

(v)   Where the word ends in a single consonant preceded by two vowels, do not double the consonant: *remain, remaining; unveil, unveiling*.

(c)   If a word ends in a consonant and *y*, change the *y* to an *i*, whether using a consonant suffix or a vowel suffix (unless the vowel is *i*, when the *y* is unchanged, to avoid a double *i*): *hazy, hazily; happy, happiness; marry, marriage; carry, carrying*.

(d)   If a word ends in *y* preceded by a vowel, the *y* is unchanged: *employ, employed, employment*.

Exercise: Try these for yourself: *necessary+ly; lazy+ness; display+ed; friendly+est; bury+ing*. Easy, isn't it? From these rules on prefixes and suffixes, you can work backwards to find the appropriate base word if necessary. If you were not sure which of *robing* or *robbing* came from *to robe*, you could use the above rules to work out *robe+ing* and *rob+ing*, which would give *robing* and *robbing*, respectively, solving your problem.

9.   **Breaking words down into their component parts** can often help with their spelling, including using your knowledge of prefixes and suffixes: *government = govern+ment; misspell = mis+spell*.

Spelling reform

There have been many calls for spelling reform, including one from philosopher Bertrand Russell. The calls have two aims which are often confused. One is to make spelling **more phonetic**, so that pronunciation follows the spelling, e.g., with no silent letters. As English has about forty-four different sounds (phonemes), that would require forty-four letters, not twenty-six, or lots of diacritical marks such as accents. There is also the big problem that words are pronounced differently in different parts of the English-speaking world. In England one could not have a phonetic spelling of *brass* which simultaneously reflected the southern long 'a', rhyming with *farce*, and the northern short 'a', rhyming with *ass*.

If one made spelling phonetic, then all words sounding alike (homophones, see page 181) would have to be spelled the same as each other (homographs, see pages 179–80), so we would lose the very useful distinctions between *rays/raze/raise*, *seamen/semen*, and *write/right/rite*, for example.

The second call is to **make spelling simpler**. The Spelling Society produced various schemes for simplification but its members could not agree which to adopt. All suggestions had weaknesses. If some radical system of spelling reform were to be adopted, people would need to learn the new system and the old one, to be able to read existing books. Anarchy and confusion would probably result.

One could not just cut out doubled consonants or doubled vowels, or we would lose the distinctions between *matting* and *mating*, *hoping* and *hopping*, *root* and *rot*, for example. As we saw earlier, doubled consonants give clues to pronunciation and vice versa, as they often make the preceding vowel sound short, as in *ammunition*.

There is a difference between
matting and *mating*.

Spelling reform would obscure the origins of words, making their meanings less clear. In summary, spelling reform might be desirable in theory, but in practice is likely to do more harm than good. Many foreigners master English spelling and pronunciation, so the British ought to be able to do so too.

Learning word origins

You do not need to know Latin or Greek to learn word origins, but learning **common roots**, whether prefixes, suffixes, or base words, is extremely useful. It helps with spellings (*anti-* or *ante-natal*? *forhead* or *forehead*?) and meanings. A word may be pronounced *benifit* but a knowledge that it comes from *bene* (Latin, *well* or *good*) helps us with the correct spelling, *benefit*.

If you look up the origin of *hypodermic* (syringe) you find that it comes from *hypo*, below or under, and *derma*, skin. You can then guess that a *hypothyroid* condition means that the thyroid gland is underactive, and that *hypothermia* implies a low body temperature.

The study of word origins – etymology – can be extremely interesting. For example, the currency unit *dollar* comes from the German *Thaler*, a shortened version of *Joachimsthaler*, a coin made from metal mined in Joachimsthal, now Jachymov in the Czech Republic.

Some words have acquired different meanings over time, as shown on pages 207–11. For example, *charity*, giving to worthy causes, is derived from the Latin *caritas*, love and affection.

Use a good dictionary to find word origins and you will soon find that you can guess the meanings of many new words just from knowing their components. Do look up any words which you do not know, to improve your vocabulary. The following list includes **common prefixes and suffixes**.

a-/an-, not, without, as in *asexual, atonal, anaemia* (deficiency of blood).

ab-, away from, off, as in *absent*; knowing that origin, you would know not to put two '*b*'s in *aberrant*, which comes from *ab+errant*, whereas *abbreviate* comes from *ab+brevis*, so has two '*b*'s.

ad-, near, to, at, as in *adrenal* (near the kidney), *adherent*. Note the difference between *adsorb*, to take onto a surface, as in *the platinum adsorbed the pollutants*, and *absorb*, to take right in, to suck in, as in *to absorb knowledge, to absorb the spillage*.

aero-, air, as in *aerobic, aerosol*.

-algia, localised pain, as in *neuralgia* (nerve pain).

amphi-, both, as in *amphibious* (living both in water and on land), *amphidextrous*.

andr-/andro-, male, as in *androgen* (male hormone), *polyandry* (having more than one husband).

ante-, before, as in *antenatal* (before birth), *antecedent, anteroom*.

anti-, opposed to, as in *antiseptic, antiwar*.

arch-, first, chief, primitive, original, as in *archbishop, archetype*.

aut-/auto-, same, self, as in *autoerotic, autoimmune, autobiography*.

bene-, well, as in *benevolent, benefit*.

bi-, twice, double, as in *bigamy, biannual, binocular*.

bio-, life, as in *biology, biography*.

card-, cardio-, heart, as in *cardiac, cardiogram*.

cent-, centi-, hundred, as in *centipede, per cent*; hundredth, as in *centimetre*.

chroma-, coloured, as in *chromatic*.

chron-, time, long, as in *chronology, chronometer*. A *chronic disease* is one going on for a long time, as opposed to an *acute* one. Some people wrongly use *chronic* to mean *acute* for a disease, although *chronic* can be used to mean *serious*.

-cide, killer, as in *matricide* (killing one's mother), *suicide, insecticide*.

circum-, around, as in *circumpolar, circumscribe*.

co-, com-, con-, joint, mutual, equal, with, as in *copilot, combine*, *conspire*. Note the usefulness of a hyphen for pronunciation and showing a word's origin: *co-proprietors* suggests an origin from *co+proprietors*, while *coproprietors* suggests a false origin from *copro-*, meaning *dung*, as in *coprophagous*, (dung-eating).

contra-, *counter-*, against, opposite, opposed to, as in *contraceptive*, *counter-espionage*.

dec-, *deca-*, ten, as in *decade*, *decapod* (having ten legs).

deci-, one tenth, as in *decimal*, *decimate*.

demi-, half, as in *demigod*, *demisemiquaver*.

-derm, skin, as in *hypodermic*, *pachyderm*, *dermatitis*.

dextro-, *dextr-*, to the right-hand side, as in *dextrocardia* (having the heart on the right-hand side of the body).

di-, two, twice, as in *dioxide*, *dicephalous* (having two heads!).

dia-, across, apart, as in *diagonal*, *diametrically*.

dys-, bad, as in *dysfunctional*, *dystrophy*.

ecto-, external, outside, as in *ectopic* (pregnancy), *ectoderm*.

-ectomy, surgical removal, as in *appendectomy*, *splenectomy*.

-ee, a suffix indicating a person receiving some action, or in a specified condition, as in *amputee*, *employee*.

endo-, inner, inside, within, as in *endoderm*, *endogenous*, *endoparasite*.

epi-, on, over, as in *epidermis*, *epigraph*.

equi-, equal, level, as in *equilateral*, *equilibrium*.

ex-, out of, former, as in *exhale*, *exorcise*, *ex-husband*.

extra-, outside, beyond, as in *extramural*, *extraordinary*.

fore-, front, before, as in *forebear* (not to be confused with *to forbear*, to refrain), *forehead*, *forecast*.

-gamy, union, marriage, as in *polygamy*, *gamete*.

gastr-, *gastro-*, stomach, as in *gastric*, *gastropod*, *gastritis*.

-gen, producing, as in *carcinogen* (substance causing cancer).

geo-, earth, as in *geology*, *geostationary*.

graph-, *-graph*, writing or drawing, as in *graphology*, *geography*, *graphics*.

gynaeco-, female, as in *gynaecology*, *gynaecocracy* (rule by women).

haem-, blood, as in *haemoglobin*, *haematology*, *haemorrhage*.

hetero-, unlike, different, as in *heterosexual*, *heterogeneous*.

homo-, alike, same, as in *homosexual*, *homogeneous*.

hydr-, *hydro-*, water, as in *hydraulics*, *hydrophobia* (fear of water).

hyper-, excessive, over, as in *hyperactive*, *hypermarket*.

hypo-, under, too little, as in *hypothermia* (too cold), *hypoallergenic*.

in-, not, as in *incompatible*, *insalubrious*.*

inter-, among, with each other, as in *interchange*, *intermarriage*.

intra-, *intro-*, within, as in *intramural*, *introspection*, *introvert*.

-itis, inflammation, as in *tonsillitis*, *tendonitis*.

kilo-, thousand, as in *kilometre*.

lact-, *lacto-*, milk, as in *lactation*, *lactose* (milk sugar).

litho-, stone, as in *monolith*, *lithography*.

* There was confusion over *inflammable*, which some people took to mean *not flammable*, as in the above usage of the prefix *in-*, and some took it to mean *flammable*, capable of being burnt. It is best to use *flammable* and *non-flammable* to avoid ambiguity.

-logy, *-ology*, subject of study, or writing, as in *musicology*, *trilogy*.

macro-, large, as in *macroscopic*, *macroeconomics*.

mal-, bad, as in *malformed*, *malignant*.

-mania, extreme desire for something, often pathologically, as in *nymphomania*, *kleptomania*.

mega-, large, million, as in *megaphone*, *megaton* (explosive power of 1 million tons of TNT).

micro-, small, as in *microscopic*, *microeconomics*.

milli-, thousand, thousandth, as in *millipede*, *millimetre*.

mono-, one, as in *monogamous*, *monotonous*.

multi-, many, as in *multiple*, *multicoloured*.

neo-, new, as in *neonate* (newborn child), *neophilia* (love of new things), *neologism*.

neuro-, nerve, as in *neurology*, *neurotic*.

non-, not, as in *nontoxic*, *nonsmoker*, *nonsense*.

octo-/octa-, eight, as in *octopus*, *octave*.

omni-, all, as in *omnivorous*, *omnidirectional*, *omnipresent*.

ortho-, straight, correct, as in *orthodox*, *orthopaedics*.

osteo-, bone, as in *osteoporosis*, *osteoarthritis*.

ot-/oto-, of the ear, as in *otic*, *otorrhoea* (discharge from the ear).

paed-, *paedo-*, *ped-*, child, as in *paediatrics*, *pederast*.

palaeo-, *paleo-*, old, ancient, as in *Palaeozoic*, *paleontology*.

pan-, all, as in *panacea*, *pantheism*.

path-, *patho-*, disease, as in *pathology*, *pathogenic*, *psychopath*.

penta-, five, as in *pentagon*, *pentaprism*.

peri-, around, as in *perimeter*, *periscope*.

phil-, *-philia*, loving, as in *philanderer*, *necrophilia*, *paedophile*.

phone-, voice, sound, as in *phonetics*, *megaphone*.

photo-, light, as in *photon*, *photography*.

-plasty, plastic surgery of a body part, as in *rhinoplasty* (nose surgery).

pod-, *-pod*, leg, feet, as in *tripod*, *podiatry*.

poly-, many, or multiple, as in *polygamy*, *polychrome*, *monopoly*.

post-, after, as in *postmortem*, *postgraduate*, *postpone*.

pre-, before, as in *prenatal*, *premature*, *prejudge*.

pro-, before, for, in favour of, substituting for, as in *progenitor*, *pro-choice*, *pronoun*, *proconsul*.

pseudo-, false, as in *pseudonym*, *pseudoscience*.

psycho-, mind, as in *psychology*, *psychopath*.

pyro-, fire, heat, as in *pyromania*, *pyrotechnic*.

quad-, four, as in *quadruped*, *quadrangle*.

quasi-, as if, like, as in *quasi-neutral*, *quasi-judicial*.

re-, back, as in *recall*, *remember*.

ren-, kidney, as in *renal*, *renitis*.

schizo-, split, as in *schizophrenia*.

semi-, half, as in *semicircular*, *semiquaver*.

sex-, six, as in *sextuplets*.

stereo-, three-dimensional or two-dimensional, as in *stereoscopic*, *stereovision*.

sub-, under, as in *submarine*, *substandard*.

super-, *sur-*, above, too much, as in *superhuman*, *superfluity*, *surfeit*.

syn-, *sym-*, together, same, as in *synchronous*, *symmetric* (from *sym* + *metric*, hence the double 'm').

tele-, at a distance, as in *telephone*, *telescope*, *television*.

tetra-, four, as in *tetrahedral*, *tetrology*.

therm-, heat, as in *thermometer*, *thermal*, *hypothermic*.

trans-, across, on the other side, beyond, as in *transpose*, *transport*, *transmit*, *transatlantic*.

tri-, three, as in *tripod*, *triumvirate*, *triple*.

ultra-, beyond, as in *ultraviolet*, *ultramodern*, *ultrasonic*.

un-, not, as in *uncomplaining*, *ungenerous*.

uni-, one, as in *unity*, *unicellular*, *unique*.

-vorous, eating, as in *carnivorous*, *omnivorous*.

Exercise on word origins (no answers are given)

- Look up the origins of *exacerbate*, *feisty*, *gear*, *laser*, *necrosis*, *normal*, *platitude*, *precocious*, *psephology*.
- From their origins, find the connection between *hysteria* and *hysterectomy*.
- Do *thesaurus* (book) and *Tyrannosaurus* (dinosaur) share a suffix?
- Look up the term *oestrous cycle* and find the surprising origin of *oestrous*.

CHAPTER 19

Sorting out word confusions

If you confuse words, it can cause misunderstandings and bring ridicule upon you. For example, people confuse *prescribed* (specified or recommended) and *proscribed* (prohibited), which have opposite meanings; with drugs, that could have life-or-death consequences. Some of the confusions listed below are made by about half the population, including undergraduates.

Fortunately, there are **easy ways** to remember which word has which meaning in many cases, as shown below. The examples are in alphabetical order of the first-named word.

Accept/except It might seem unlikely that anyone could confuse *to accept*, to take or receive something offered, with *to except*, to exclude, but people do. An advertisement for Barclays Bank offered to *except* cheques.

'We except cheques.'

Affect/effect These have totally different meanings. As **nouns**, you will usually meet *an effect*, a result from some cause. An *affect* is a psychological term for an emotion associated with an idea. The important confusion arises when these words are **verbs**. *To effect* is to bring something about, to bring to completion. *To affect* is to have some influence on. If you were drowning and I *effected* your rescue, your rescue would have been fully accomplished. If I had *affected* your rescue, I would have merely influenced it.

A student wrote that *Bad diet effects a woman's pregnancy*, meaning that bad diet makes a woman pregnant, which is rubbish. Similarly, *Global warming effects crop yields* is nonsense. One way to remember the difference between the verbs is that if something has been *effected*, it has had the complete *effect*.

a.m./p.m. These stand for *ante* (before) *meridiem* and *post* (after) *meridiem*, from *meridies*, Latin for *midday*. The confusion comes when people write 12 a.m. or 12 p.m., both of which should mean midnight, being twelve hours before or after midday. **Using 12 p.m. for midday** is a particularly common error although some claim that it is an accepted usage. It is best to **write 12 noon or 12 midnight**, to avoid ambiguity.

As/like Authorities differ on what is acceptable. It is best to use *like* before nouns and pronouns, and *as* as a conjunction before phrases and clauses:

> *We go to the pub on Friday evenings **as** we used to when students.* [That seems fine]

> *We go to the pub on Friday evenings **like** we used to when students.* [That jars]

Elements of Style, by Strunk and White, 4th edition, is eloquent on this point and makes an excellent observation on language change:

> Like *has long been widely used by the illiterate; lately it has been taken up by the knowing and the well-informed, who find it catchy, or liberating, and who use it as though they were slumming. If every word or device that achieved currency were immediately authenticated, simply on the ground of popularity, the language would be as chaotic as a ball game with no foul lines . . . The most useful thing to know about* like *is that most carefully edited publications regard its use before phrases and clauses as simple error.*

Assume/deduce You *assume* from experience or theory, but you *deduce* from facts or data. *I **assume** that you are educated because you went to a good school. I **deduce** that you are educated because you show such a wide range of knowledge.*

Biannual/biennial *Biannual* events occur twice a year, from *bi-*, twice, *-annual*, a year, but *biennial* events happen every two years. *Biennial* has an *e*, as does *every*.

Complimentary/complementary Things are *complementary* if they *complete* each other, both words having an 'e' after the 'l'. *Their skills were complementary; she was good at navigation, he at driving. Complimentary* relates to *compliments*, remarks expressing admiration. *He was complimentary about my new dress. Complimentary* also means *without payment. I was given complimentary tickets for the play.*

Defuse/diffuse As verbs, *defuse* means *remove a triggering device*, or *calm* [a situation], while *diffuse* means *spread out*.

Discrete/discreet *Discrete* means separate, as in *discrete particles* or *discrete amounts*. *Discreet* means *prudent, secret, tactful*, as in *The wife's lover was very discreet and avoided detection*. The difference can be remembered from the way the words end, in *'t'* for *discreet, prudent* and *secret*, and in *'te'* for *discrete* and *separate*. In *discrete*, meaning separate, the two *'e'*s are separated.

Disinterested/uninterested *Disinterested* means unbiased, impartial, but *uninterested* means not interested, bored. Referees should be *disinterested* in the game's result, but should not be *uninterested* in their duties.

Ensure/insure *Ensure* means *make certain; insure* means *cover against risk*.

Fewer/less The confusion arises as both are opposites of *more*. *Fewer* means fewer in number where the items are distinct, discrete and discontinuous. *There were fewer than six boys present.* *Less* relates to amounts which can vary by small degrees, not just by whole numbers. *Joan weighed less than Mary.* One would use *less hot, less money*, not *fewer hot* or *fewer money*. One could have *fewer coins* or *fewer worries*. A supermarket was persuaded to change the signs *Five items or less* to *Five items or fewer*, which is correct.

Contrast the following:

There were fewer beautiful women present.

There were less beautiful women present.

In the first statement, *fewer* is an adjective, qualifying *women*. In the second statement, *less* is an adverb, qualifying the adjective *beautiful*, not conveying how many were present.

Fortuitous/fortunate *Fortuitous* means *by chance; fortunate* means *lucky*.

In/into; on/onto *In* and *on* indicate locations, while *into* and *onto* show directions of motion. *She was in the bathroom and climbed into the bath. He was on the ladder and climbed onto the roof.*

Infer/imply/confer Only a mind can *infer* something, making a deduction. Data can never *infer*, as data have no brain. The data can *imply* something, suggest something, without any conscious intention. To *confer* means to *consult*, as in *confer with colleagues*, or *bestow*, as in *confer a knighthood*.

*I **inferred** from the data on wheat yields that wind speed was less important than temperature. The data **implied** that damage by birds was more important than losses from rats.*

Lay/lie *Lay* is transitive but *lie* is intransitive: *The hen **lays** an egg most mornings. We **lie** down to sleep.* I object when told to *lay* on the chiropractor's couch. Lay what?

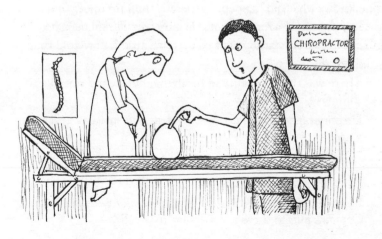

May/can *May I?* requests permission. *Can I?* asks whether I am able to do something. My limerick illustrates the difference:

May and Can

A lover of English named Ann
Asked: 'Please may I sleep with this man?'
When told: 'No, you can't!'
She replied: 'But dear aunt,
Experience proves that I can!'

In ordinary speech, it is usual to ask: *'Can I come in?'*, although *'May I come in?'* is correct if permission to enter is being requested.

May/might This is not a straightforward distinction, as *might* is the past tense and the subjunctive of *may*. *He might have come last night* means that it was possible for him to have come last night, but could also be the subjunctive (see pages 54–5), a supposition that he might have come, and possibly did so. *He may have come last night* has a similar meaning. One must not use *may* if one knows what did happen, as there is then no uncertainty.

It is definitely wrong to put: *He **may** have died in the road accident, but survived with minor injuries*, because we are told that he did not die.

There was the possibility of his dying, but he did not die, so the subjunctive, *might*, is needed:

*He **might** have died in the road accident, but survived with minor injuries.*

An idiocy sometimes seen on packets of nuts is the safety warning: *May contain nuts*. That is nuts. It should read *Contains nuts* as there is no doubt involved.

May be/maybe *Maybe* is an adverb meaning *perhaps*, whereas *may be* is a combination of two verbs. *Maybe we will go to Scotland on Sunday. It may be cold in Inverness.*

Past/passed *Passed* is from the verb *to pass*, with the *-ed* ending showing the past tense: *He **passed** his exams. Past* is not a verb but is an adjective (*the **past** tense*), an adverb (*the jet flew **past***), a noun (*the **past** has a long history*) and a preposition (*She ran **past** her school*).

Practice/practise, licence/license, device/devise, advice/ advise In British English, *practice, licence, device* and *advice* are nouns, while *practise, license, devise* and *advise* are verbs. In the first two pairs of words, the nouns and verbs are pronounced the same, but *advice* and *device* rhyme with *vice* while *advise* and *devise* rhyme with *lies*. By remembering the pronunciations of *advice* and *advise*, and *device* and *devise*, one can work out which are nouns and which are verbs for any of these pairs of words, and hence the spelling.

Principal/principle *Principal* means *head* or *chief*, as an adjective or noun. *Principle* is a noun meaning a rule, fundamental truth or ethical guide. The difference can be remembered from:

My pal, the Principal, had multiple principles.

Programme/program In British English, we distinguish between *programme*, a schedule or a description of a play and its performers, and *program*, instructions for a computer. The Americans use *program* for both.

Sight/site/cite *Sight*, to do with seeing, requires *light*, which is spelled the same way. *Site* can be a verb, to place something somewhere, or a noun, a place where something is *situated*. Its meaning is clear from *situation*. To *cite* is to quote, as in *citation*.

Stationary/stationery *Stationary* means *static*, not moving, while *stationery* includes writing materials such as paper, envelopes and pens. The difference is easily remembered from all the '*a*'s in *Ma's car was stationary* and all the '*e*'s in *The envelopes were stationery*.

That/which When these words are used as relative pronouns, they tend to be used interchangeably in speech and in informal writing. They usually introduce subordinate clauses telling us more about a preceding noun. For formal use, authorities sometimes give different rules as to when each word should be used. The best advice is to use **that** in restrictive clauses and **which** in non-restrictive clauses.

What does that mean? In *The plane that is on the runway is painted in lurid colours*, the clause *that is on the runway* identifies a particular plane, restricting the clause *is painted in lurid colours* to that plane. In *The plane, which is on the runway, is painted in lurid colours*, the clause *which is on the runway* does not define which plane is being referred to. If the clause introduced by the relative pronoun is set off in commas, *which* is probably the right word to use as a pair of commas are usually used to set off non-restrictive clauses.

Do not use *that* to introduce non-restrictive clauses, so that *The plane, that is on the runway, is painted in lurid colours* is wrong. In restrictive clauses, *that* is preferred, but *which* is often considered acceptable as well: *The plane which is on the runway is painted in lurid colours*. Does that look acceptable to you?

There/their/they're These sound alike and are easily distinguished because *there*, to do with place, contains the word *here*, as does *where*; *their*, the possessive of *they*, contains the word *heir*, someone who will possess something later. The apostrophe in *they're* shows it to be a contraction of *they are*.

Two/to/too *Two* is a number; *to* is a preposition or adverb, while *too* is an adverb meaning *as well*, or *excessive*. **Two** men *came* **to** *the door, then a woman came* **too**.

Weather/whether/wether *Wether* has a letter missing compared to the other two words, and means a male sheep, especially a castrated one (something missing!). *Weather* is to do with temperature and rain and *whether* is a conjunction introducing alternatives: *We do not know whether the weather will be fine or dismal.*

Where/wear/were/we're The first two words sound fairly alike, ending in an *-air* sound, while *were* and *we're* end in an *-er* sound. *Where* involves place, as shown by its containing the word *here*, while *were* is the past tense of *was*. *Wear* is to do with clothing, as in *When it is noisy, wear ear protectors*, or to do with abrasion, as in *wear and tear*. The apostrophe in *we're* shows that it is a contraction of *we are*.

Which/who Use *who* for humans, *which* for everything else, whether living or not. *The man who came home . . . Jane, who was out . . . The cat which mewed . . . The tree which fell . . .*

Whose/who's *Whose* is the possessive form of *who*, while *who's* is a contraction of *who is* or *who has*. **Who's** going to tell me **whose** car hit mine?

CHAPTER 20

Onyms, homos and heteros

This unconventional heading covers important concepts. It helps to have names for discussing them, and to know their practical use. The names have word origins which describe them well.

Acronyms

Acronyms are pronounceable names made from initial letters or parts of words. The term comes from *acro-*, a prefix meaning beginning, edge, summit, with the suffix *-onym*, meaning word or name. Thus *NATO* is the **N**orth **A**tlantic **T**reaty **O**rganization, and *AIDS* stands for **a**cquired **i**mmune **d**eficiency **s**yndrome. The German acronym *Nazi* stands for **Na**tional**so**zialist, a member of the National Socialist German Workers' Party.

It is best to have acronyms **entirely in capital letters** to distinguish them from confusable ordinary words. Because of capital letters, we can distinguish an *It* girl (young female celebrity) from an *IT* girl (one dealing with information technology). The capitals in *AIDS* distinguish the disease from *aids* (as in *hearing aids* or *she aids her neighbours*).

Some acronyms have become ordinary words and are put in **lower-case letters**, such as *radar* (**ra**dio **d**etection **a**nd **r**anging).

Do not explain an acronym if it is common, such as *AIDS*. If it is unusual or one you have coined, then explain it the first time that you use it in a piece, giving all the words in full. If an expression is used only once in your piece, there may be no need for an acronym when you can give the full words.

Synonyms

Synonyms have the same or a very close meaning. The word comes from *syn-*, associated, together, with *-onym*. Words with slightly different meanings are near-synonyms, which are more common than exact ones. Words may be synonyms in one meaning, as in *escapade/lark*, when *lark* is an escapade, but the two words are not synonyms when *lark* is a bird.

Thesauruses and dictionaries of synonyms can be very useful for getting variety into a piece, or to avoid repeating a word too soon after its previous use (see pages 61–2). Using such aids can help you to find a better, more exact or expressive word than the one you first thought of. Most spell-checkers have a synonym facility.

Antonyms

Antonyms have the opposite meaning. The word comes from *anti-*, against, opposing, with *-onym*. Because *right/wrong* are antonyms and so are *right/left*, one cannot deduce that *wrong* and *left* are synonyms, because the word *right* has more than one meaning.

There are many **prefixes** used to provide **negative forms** of nouns, verbs, adjectives and adverbs, as in *undress*, *dismount*, *mislead*, *decompose*, *unnaturally*, *dishonest*, *immoral*, *illegitimate*, *inactive*, *ignoble*, *irreligious*, *nonaggression*.

You might use antonyms when weighing up two sides of an argument, or when making contrasts. Thinking about a word's opposite can help to clarify meanings.

Onyms

Onym: the word exists but is rare. It means *name* or *word* but is usually just a suffix, *-onym*. *Onymous*, used of a book, means bearing the author's name, the antonym of *anonymous*. An **anonym** is an anonymous person or publication, or can mean a pseudonym.

Pseudonyms

Pseudonyms are adopted fictitious names, especially by authors, some of whom write under more than one name. The word comes from *pseudo-*, false, with *-onym*. Nom de plume means the same thing. Agatha Christie wrote romantic novels under the name Mary Westmacott. Stephen King wrote four novels as Richard Bachman because his publishers were worried that the public would not buy more than one novel a year from a single author.

Pseudonyms are sometimes used for competition entries, so that judges cannot identify whose entries they are judging. Use a pseudonym only if you have a special reason to do so.

Eponyms

Eponyms are names, such as of places, usually derived from a person's name. Thus *Constantinople* is an eponym, with the city named after the Roman Emperor *Constantine*. The term *Brussels sprouts* demonstrates an eponym based on a place, not a person. They are named after the city of Brussels where sprouts became popular in the sixteenth century. The word eponym can also refer to the person or persons after whom a place, play or period is named (e.g., the *Georgian* period, 1714–1830, named after Kings George I, II, III and IV). *Hamlet* is the eponymous protagonist of Shakespeare's play, *Hamlet*.

Homonyms

Homonyms are words with the same pronunciation and spelling but which are unrelated in origin. The word comes from Greek *homo-*, the same or alike, with *-onym*. Examples include *fair* (just)/ *fair* (as at a fairground), and *lead* (noun, as of a dog)/*lead* (verb, go ahead). The word *Pole*, a person from Poland, would not be a homonym of *pole*, as it has a capital letter, but *pole* (telegraph pole) and *pole* (geographical term) are homonyms.

Homographs

Homographs are words with the same spelling but different meanings; they may be pronounced the same (homophones) or differently (heterophones). The word comes from *homo-*, the same or alike, and *-graph*, writing or drawing. Examples with different pronunciation include *sow* (plant seeds, pronounced 'so') and *sow* (female pig, rhyming with 'now'), and *wound* (injury, pronounced

'*woond*') and *wound* (wrapped around, pronounced '*wound*').
Examples of homographs which are also homophones include
row (as in a boat) and *row* (as in a line), both rhyming with 'hoe',
whereas another homograph, *row* (a quarrel) rhymes with 'cow',
so is a heterophone of the other two *rows*.

It is easy to find homographs in a dictionary as headwords
for the main meaning are often followed by a series of different
homographs with different meanings.

You may use homographs in written jokes, and need to
be aware of homographs in case you use a word with double
meanings and might be misunderstood.

To sort out homographs, use your knowledge of the people
or the context. If a man writes to you that he and his wife
have 'had a terrific row', you can probably guess whether they
quarrelled violently or enjoyed pulling on oars.

🎗 Homophones

Homophones are words which sound alike. The word comes from *homo-* with *-phone*, indicating speech, sound or voice. Many homophones are spelled differently (heterographs), as in *flee/flea*, *lead* (metal)/*led* (past tense of *to lead*), *feet/feat*, *meet/meat*, *no/know*, *stare/stair*, *by/buy/bye*, *bawd/bored/board*, *bier/beer* and *none/nun*.

The noun *practice* and the verb *practise* are homophones, but *advice* (noun, rhymes with '*vice*') and *advise* (verb, rhymes with '*lies*') are not homophones. Thinking of the pronunciations of the noun *advice* and the verb *advise* helps with spelling the nouns *licence* and *practice* and the verbs *license* and *practise*.

Homophones are used in puns and in other kinds of joke. You need to be aware of homophones so that your spoken words are not misinterpreted. A lady was telling me about the obliging staff at a particular pub. I thought that she said that they would get one a *hooker* (prostitute) if asked, but when I queried this, she swore that she had said *hookah* (oriental pipe)!

To sort out homophones, use your knowledge of the people or the context. Thus *AIDS*, *aides*, *aids* (verb) and *aids* (plural noun) are all homophones; they can often be distinguished by the listener applying context, position and grammar.

🎗 Heterophones

Heterophones are words with different meanings which are spelled the same (homographs) but pronounced differently. The word comes from *hetero-*, different, another, with *-phone*, sound. Examples are *bow* (for shooting arrows, rhyming with 'owe') and *bow* (incline the head, rhyming with 'cow'), and *read* (present tense of *to read*, pronounced 'reed') and *read* (past tense of *to read*, pronounced 'red').

Jokes

Puns involve homophones, homographs, heterophones and heterographs. See also the chapter on humour in English (pages 212–18). Here are some examples.

> *What do auctioneers need to know?*

The answer is *Lots!* That is a pun with homographs and homophones, as the answer can mean *many facts* or *a set of items to be auctioned*. That joke works on paper and when spoken.

> *'I'd like to see your mother, please,' said the teacher when Alice opened the door.*
>
> *'She ain't 'ere miss,' Alice replied.*
>
> *'Why, Alice, where's your grammar?' the teacher asked.*
>
> *'She ain't 'ere neither, miss,' said Alice.*

This involves homophones and heterographs, but the word *grandma* is not actually written. That joke works on paper and when spoken.

Exercise (no answers are given)

- Say out loud the words *wine* and *whine*. In your pronunciation, are they homophones?
- Think of two homophones each for *byte* and *sight*; a synonym for *shovel*, and an antonym for *immigration*.

- Give a homonym for *soil* (earth), and a homograph for *beat* (thrash).
- Analyse how particular puns work in jokes which you know: do they work equally well in speech and on paper?

CHAPTER 21

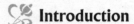

Business writing

Introduction

Even if we do not do any business writing, we receive it and need to understand it.

The main purpose of business writing is **to communicate**, and plain simple words are best. Unfortunately, when faced with doing it, many people behave as if plain everyday language does not exist.

The important part is **gathering and organising the material**. If there is insufficient, you tend to 'pad'. If there is too much, you may become overwhelmed by the task of getting it all in.

The important principles are:

Clarity – Simplicity – Brevity

If your writing is 'weird and wonderful' it will not be **clear**, neither will it be **simple** enough to understand easily. If you 'pad', **brevity**, the essence of good writing, will be lost.

Getting started

Here are some ideas to help you get started:

- **Let rough ideas take form in your mind**. Often we cannot start because the thoughts we want to express are not clear in our own mind. Give yourself time to let your ideas 'simmer', but don't use this as an excuse to put off getting down to writing.
- **Talk to other people about your ideas**. Discussing your thoughts and plans will often bring out new ideas, and will help you form your ideas more clearly.
- **Write as you think**. To get started, just 'dump' all your thoughts down on paper or screen in an unstructured way. Keep the ideas flowing. Offload your thoughts in brief note form so there is not too much to write. Then go over what you have done so far. Use it to create an ordered, logical outline structure.
- **Write visually**. It may help to put your thoughts down using diagrams such as flowcharts, sketches or 'mind maps'. Words are not the only way to get your ideas on paper. Go back over your 'visuals' and use them to create an ordered outline structure of what you plan to write.
- **Write – don't edit**. Grammar, punctuation and spelling are initially not important. Getting ideas down is the first step. Tidy up the writing later.

Style

All writing should be readable and interesting, and communicate its message clearly and unambiguously.

Lee Iacocca, the former Chief Executive of Chrysler, was definitely against trying to impress by style. There is a paragraph in his autobiography which is particularly apt:

> *Say it in English, and keep it short. I once read a 15-page paper that was tough to understand. I called in the author and asked him to explain what was in the tome he had written. He did it in two minutes flat. He identified what we were doing wrong, what we could do to fix it, and what he recommended. When he finished I asked him why he didn't write in the paper the way he'd just said it to me. He didn't have an answer. All he said was: 'I was taught that way.'*

Iacocca's wisdom is a guide to all writers: keep it simple, keep it short.

The **main styles** can be divided into three broad classifications:

- **Formal**: *The newly inaugurated copying system has enjoyed a most favourable reception.*
- **Friendly**: *Our new copying system is just great.*
- **Familiar**: *Our new copying system has become very popular with the departments that use it.*

The more formal the style, the more likely we are to use less familiar words and less simple verb forms – such as the passive voice. At the other extreme, the familiar style might drop into slang and incomplete sentences.

The choice of style is a matter of individual preference, organisational custom and – most importantly – the feelings and expectations of your reader(s). Business readers today prefer shorter, more easily readable writing; the friendly style is probably best.

Here are some common pitfalls to avoid:

SUPERFLUOUS WORDS

It is easy to add words that contribute nothing, repeating a meaning already given, for example:

- 'staff of suitable *calibre* and *quality*' (Overemphasis and confusion of meaning.)
- 'I personally believe . . .' (Who else believes?)

Another common fault is unnecessary adjectives and adverbs:

- *true* facts   (If it is a fact it is true.)
- *actively* investigate   (Can you investigate passively?)
- I *would* suggest   (If you mean it, why be tentative?)
- *completely* fatal   (Can something be half fatal?)

Edit out such banalities.

POMPOUS PHRASES

Avoid pointless jargon. Many of the phrases are clichés (see pages 143–4) that we use unthinkingly:

- 'further to the above'
- 'the aforementioned'
- 'at this moment in time'
- 'at the end of the day'
- 'in the not too distant future'

Seek out and delete these and similar phrases.

VAGUE, ABSTRACT WORDS AND PHRASES

Using long-winded phrases leads to vagueness. Be specific.
Do not write:

> *It was suggested that consideration be given to the possibility of*
> *improvement in our facilities for conferences with the object*
> *of elimination of noise and provision of adequate ventilation.*

if you can write:

> *We need a better place to meet. This room is hot and noisy.*

The more directly you express yourself, the happier your readers
will be.

'HEDGING'

Words such as 'perhaps', 'probably', 'comparatively', are used
by writers to avoid committing themselves. If that is your
intention, then all right. However, if it is not intended, it
destroys conviction. Avoid vague adjectives and adverbs, such
as 'appreciable', 'substantial', 'soon' if you can use specific figures,
dates, times and so on. In this example, the *italicised* words 'hedge':

> Additional evidence *suggests* that the difference in the
> midrange of the curves *may possibly indicate* a curve form that
> our hypothesis *may not adequately* encompass.

THE PROXIMITY RULE

Keep modifying words or phrases close to the word or phrase they
modify, otherwise your meaning may be uncertain. For example:

> *A discussion was held on overtime working in the office.*

What went on in the office – the discussion or the overtime working? Or was the discussion held while the staff were on overtime? Make the meaning quite clear; rewrite the sentence – even if it becomes a bit longer – and use punctuation. For example:

> *A discussion, on overtime working, was held in the office.*

Do not write that
> *The work area needs cleaning badly.*

when you mean
> *The work area badly needs cleaning.*

Misplaced modifiers can be amusing but may make you look foolish:

> *The fire was extinguished before any damage was done by the fire brigade.*

> *He told her that he wanted to marry her frequently.*

MISUSE OF PRONOUNS

Be careful not to use pronouns which could apply to different nouns. For example:

> *Mary told Susan she was being promoted.*

Who was being promoted?

> *The car collided with the van at the crossroads. It had to be towed away to avoid a traffic jam.*

What had to be towed away?

WORDS WITH SEVERAL MEANINGS

Words that have two or more meanings may leave the reader in doubt about your message. For example:

> *We* **dispense** *with accuracy.*

> *It is* **practically** *done.*

> *His action was* **sanctioned**.

The context is often a clue to the meaning intended. Use a synonym without ambiguity if possible, e.g., *almost* instead of *practically* in the second example.

DOUBLE NEGATIVES AND NEGATIVE CONSTRUCTIONS

Try to phrase your message in a positive way rather than a negative one. Instead of:

> *A decision should not be delayed.*

write

> *A decision should be made.*

Try to avoid confusing multiple negatives, such as:

> *There is no reason to doubt that it is not true.*

Memos (Memoranda)

PURPOSE

The purpose of a memo is to communicate as briefly as possible so that prompt action will follow.

THE IMPORTANCE OF MEMOS

The memo is essential in most organisations. Messages need to be sent from one person to another, giving instructions, requesting information, confirming arrangements.

For certain purposes, memos are usually better than telephone calls or face-to-face communication, for example:

- to transmit exactly the same information to several people;
- to confirm the time, date and place of a meeting to a number of people;
- to put on record the information, policies or decisions reached at a meeting or conference;
- to confirm, as a matter of record, a decision or agreement;
- to transmit information, policies or directives to an individual.

TOPIC

A memo should relate to **one topic** only. Do not combine messages on several topics in a single memo or some may be overlooked. We are selective in attention and we prioritise.

SEQUENCING

Memos should present information in a sequence that is easy and logical for the reader to understand. There should be:

- an introductory sentence or paragraph stating its purpose;
- the main points set out in simple direct sentences, using numbers or bullet points. Longer memos should be set out in clear paragraphs, each dealing with a specific aspect of the topic;
- a concluding sentence or paragraph identifying what action the reader needs to take, and when.

All memos should:

- give the date and reference number (where applicable);
- indicate sender and recipient(s);
- give subject headings;
- deal with each point in a separate paragraph;
- indicate clearly what action is required;
- indicate who is responsible for carrying this out.

Letters

There are many ways of transmitting the written word – on paper by 'snail mail'; telephonically by fax – or even by 'text'; or electronically by e-mail. Whatever method is used, the principles of good writing always apply and can be quickly learned. Write your message **as clearly as you can**.

Because you know to whom you are writing, you can adapt your style to their needs. If you receive a letter in old-fashioned pompous 'officialese', you don't have to respond similarly. Write back in a clear conversational style – show them a good example! Get to know your readers – watch for their reaction.

The key to good letter writing is courtesy:

- Always answer letters promptly.
- Get your correspondent's name and title correct.
- Be considerate and sincere.

THE FIVE 'Cs'

Be clear. Avoid ambiguities; use correct punctuation; place adjectives and adverbs in the right context.

Be concise. Brevity means selecting the right words; eliminate 'padding' caused by hackneyed clichés; cut out jargon and 'commercialese'!

Be correct. Ensure your facts, figures, data, detail and all information are correct. Be sure that grammar, punctuation and especially spelling are correct.

Be complete. Provide all the information or answers to satisfy both the reader and the purpose of the letter. If there are enclosures – enclose them!

Be courteous. Choose words to create the right tone which will convey the 'image' to the reader of a warm, helpful, interested human being.

🌿 Fax

To be effective a fax should be short – yards of fax paper are a deterrent to reading. Always head a fax with the subject and the addressee's name, rather like a memo. It is not necessary to set out the name and address at the top left.

The greeting, body of the letter and salutation should follow the usual letter-writing rules. The fax format gives you the opportunity to move straight to the point of the communication. Be brief, but not terse, cutting out the outdated 'commercialese' often found in business letters.

🌿 E-mail

Business communication is about getting your message across clearly and professionally.

Write e-mail letters as you would write a normal business letter and ask yourself: 'How would I feel if I received this message?'

E-mail offers the opportunity for rapid exchange of views and information. If this is the case then one may omit formal openings and closings of each exchange, especially if your respondent does so first. In negotiations by e-mail it is vital to be sure that mutual understanding exists. The e-mail exchange can continue rapidly until both sides are satisfied that they have reached acceptable agreement.

E-mail is global but has not yet broken down business etiquette barriers, so generally start formally with 'Dear Mr X', not 'Hi there!' Never address someone by their first name unless you have established a personal relationship, even if only by letter or phone. Doing business by e-mail can seem impersonal, so making contact by phone as well is a good way to build your relationship.

Reply to e-mails promptly. A swift 'I'll get back to you' is better than silence.

Remember that e-mail is not private, at least not when sent unencrypted. If there is confidential or sensitive material, a private letter may be better. Add confidentiality or security notices to your e-mails if you are not sure who may read them.

It is extremely frustrating to receive e-mails which mention an **attachment** which is actually missing. Double-check that all intended attachments are attached.

Error-spotting exercise

This is loosely based on real business documents from one firm, with the name and phone numbers changed. Note any errors or omissions, but do not worry about omissions of words such as *the* from such a summary document.

B. Z BUILDING SERVICES
U.K
TEL 0800 914 7913 MOB 0790067785
CUSTOMERS DETAILS
DESCIPTION OF WORK

1. *To take out lose bricks on back of property were needed.*
2. *To supply and lay new bricks maching in with old.*
3. *To supply and coat bricks with p.v.a.*
4. *To repair guttering where needed.*
5. *To re coat walls with t.m.c. fine textured wall coating where windows have been replaced. Colour of coating waterlily*
7. *New step to be re built*

TOTAL £3.500
DEPOSIT £1.500 RECIEVED
OUSTANDING £2.000

All work as been carried out to customers satisfaction

ALL WORK CARRYS A 15 YEAR GUARANTEE FROM DATE OF COMPLETION

❦ Answer to error-spotting exercise

There is no address and no name of the originator of this document. How could one enforce a guarantee against a phone number?

In such documents, the omission of definite or indefinite articles does not matter.

The first two lines have a full stop missing after the second letter. Either both letters in acronyms such as *UK* should have full stops after them, or neither letter should have a full stop. In the mobile phone number, the final digit was missing, so my phone call did not get through.

The apostrophe is missing from CUSTOMERS, and an 'R' from DESCIPTION.

1. should have *loose* and *where*.
2. should have *matching*.
5. should have *recoat* and *fine-textured*.
5 and 7 lack the full stops used after the other items.
7. should be number 6, and have *rebuilt*.

The three amounts of money have a full stop where a comma is required, changing the amounts one-thousand-fold.

RECIEVED should be *RECEIVED*.
OUSTANDING lacks a 'T'.
as should be *has*.
customers lacks an apostrophe.
CARRYS should be *CARRIES*.
There should be a hyphen between *15* and *YEAR*.

CHAPTER 22

Using foreign words, phrases and accents

It is important to understand frequently used **foreign words and phrases**, so that you are not caught out if someone else uses them. If you employ foreign expressions, use only those which your readers are likely to understand, or it will seem like showing off.

Sometimes a foreign word or phrase expresses a thought better than any English one: it is the *mot juste* (the most appropriate word), conferring a certain *cachet* (prestige), but using it is not *de rigueur* (required by etiquette).

English derives from many sources, including Latin, Greek, French, German and Asian languages. It is still taking words from other languages, so it can be a matter of opinion as to what constitutes a foreign word.

The *Collins English Dictionary*, 6th edition, has some words and phrases of foreign origin in normal type, such as *kindergarten* (German, school for the very young) and *esprit de corps* (French, sense of shared pride or purpose), suggesting that they have been assimilated into English, whereas *Schadenfreude* (German, pleasure in another's misfortune) is given in italics with an initial capital letter, as if not firmly established in English. Terms such as *attaché* and *café* are shown as assimilated but still need those accents in English.

Diacritical marks are signs placed above or below a letter or syllable to indicate a change in pronunciation, in the length of vowel sounds, or to indicate the stress on a syllable. They include **accents** such as the **acute** ['] as on *é*, the **grave** [`] as on *è*, the **circumflex** [^] as on *ê*, and the **cedilla** [¸] as under *ç*. The **tilde** [~], as on *ñ*, changes the *n* sound to *ny*, so that *mañana* (Spanish, tomorrow or morning) is pronounced *manyana*.

The **diaeresis** is a mark [¨] placed over the second of two consecutive vowels to indicate that that vowel is pronounced separately, as in *naïve* (pronounced *nigh-eve*). Word-processing programs will sometimes automatically put on the correct diacritical marks, as in *naïve*.

The French acute and grave accents change the sound of the vowel, whereas the circumflex usually indicates a missing letter 's': *forêt* means *forest* and *hâte* means *haste*, not *hate*. The German **umlaut**, as in *ä* and *ü*, changes the vowel sound. Thus *Frau* (married woman) is pronounced *frow*, but *Fräulein* (unmarried woman) is pronounced *froy-line*.

In poetry one may get what looks like a grave accent over a vowel to indicate that the vowel should be pronounced, as in *time's wingèd chariot*, where *wingèd* is to be pronounced as two syllables *wing-ed*, not *wingd*. Other symbols in poetry indicate stressed ['] and unstressed [˘] syllables. The latter mark is the **breve**.

In some cases, accents are definitely needed to distinguish a foreign word from an English one. Contrast *pâté* (food) with *pate* (the head, especially in relation to baldness). A student gave me a document headed *Resume*: he meant *Résumé*, a life summary.

If you mark words as foreign by putting them in italics, put them as they would be in the foreign language, with accents, initial capital letters for German nouns, etc. If you put them as assimilated into English, in non-italic characters, some still need the accents, as in crèche, fiancé, protégé, cliché, blasé and risqué.

If a word has more than one accent in the foreign language, you must put all or none of them: *tête-à-tête* (French, a cosy meeting of two people, literally head-to-head) needs all three accents or none, preferably three. A newspaper had an odd German-English hybrid word, with no italics: 'über-fresh', meaning ultra-fresh, and young people sometimes use phrases such as *über cool*.

To see what a difference using italics makes for foreign phrases, compare these alternatives:

He has been called the enfant terrible of the violin.

He has been called the *enfant terrible* of the violin.

One might read the first version as *en-fant terribull*, as if it were English, but the second suggests immediately that it should be read with the French pronunciation, *on-fon tereeble*.

Two common Latin abbreviations are *e.g.* (*exempli gratia*, for example) and *i.e.* (*id est*, that is). They used to be put in italics as foreign but that is rarely done now. They should have both full stops, showing that they are abbreviations, not strange short words. Some newspapers omit both full stops; it is even worse to put only a final full stop. Where you would put a comma after *for example*, as in *for example, an elephant*, then put one after *e.g.* or *i.e.*, too.

If you need foreign accents in a **word-processed document** when using Microsoft Windows, you can find extended character sets using Start > All Programs > Accessories > System Tools > Character Map, then choosing the font required and scrolling down to the desired character. This can be selected, copied [Ctrl C] and pasted [Ctrl V]. There is also a Unicode system for many characters; this is explained in the Help advice for the Character Map. If you are going to use accents several times, you can put the Character Map on screen, then minimise and maximise it as required, or just copy and paste a previously used accented letter.

Alternatively, one can put on Num Lock, then press ALT with one of the following numbers on the right-hand number pad: 0224 for à, 0225 for á, 0226 for â, 0232 for è, 0233 for é, 0234 for ê, 0241 for ñ, 0228 for ä, 0235 for ë, 0239 for ï, 0246 for ö, 0252 for ü, 0244 for ô, 0251 for û. Greek, Cyrillic, Arabic, Hebrew, Sinhala, Farsi, Hindi and other scripts can be obtained, but with other languages, keyboards may have some letters in different places.

Some hand-held computing devices and laptops do not have Num Lock or the right-hand number pad but can still produce foreign accents using the **Ctrl key**, which can be done with other computers, too. Ctrl ' [apostrophe], then the letter, e.g., *a*, gives an acute accent over the letter: á, é, í, etc. Ctrl ` [top row, left end], then the letter, gives grave accents: à, è, etc. Ctrl + Shift ^ then the letter gives â, ô, etc. Ctrl + Shift : [colon] then the letter gives ä, ü, etc. Ctrl + Shift ~ [tilde] gives ñ, ã, etc. The capital letter versions are obtained by using an extra Shift, as in Ctrl + Shift : [colon] + Shift u gives Ü. Ctrl , [comma] + c gives ç.

Here are **some foreign words and phrases worth knowing**, but the list is far from exhaustive.

French: *à la mode* (fashionable), *au fait* [with] (fully informed about something), *au revoir* (goodbye), *badinage* (banter), *beau monde* (fashionable society), *décolletage* (low-cut neckline on women's clothing), *double entendre* (something which can be interpreted in two ways, one of them dirty), *femme fatale* (seductive woman with a bad effect on men), *né*, *née* (male and female respectively, born, as put on forms for a woman's maiden name), *protégé* (*protégée* if female; a person helped by a patron); *raison d'être* (reason for living); *recherché* (refined, known only to connoisseurs); *risqué* (almost indecent); R.S.V.P. (*répondez s'il vous plaît*, please reply).

German: There are assimilated war-related terms which are not given an initial capital letter, including *flak* (an acronym for anti-aircraft fire) and *blitzkrieg* (lightning war). *U-boat* retains its capital letter, as do *Sturm und Drang* (Storm and Stress). Other words keeping the capital letter include *Doppelgänger* (double in the sense of a look-alike), *Übermensch* (superman) and *Zeitgeist* (spirit of the age). Musical terms include *Lieder* (songs).

Greek: *hoi polloi* (the common people).

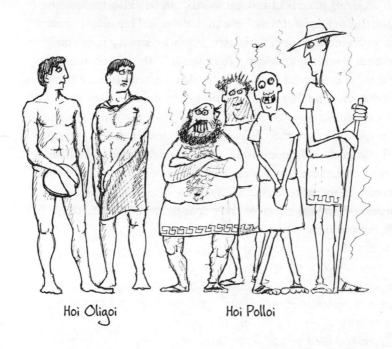

Hoi Oligoi   Hoi Polloi

Italian: many culinary and musical terms, such as *pizza*, *al dente* (cooked but firm) and *lento* (slowly); *piazza* (open town square). Of these, only *al dente* is usually printed in italics, with the rest treated as assimilated into English.

Latin: *ad hoc* (for a particular purpose, like a committee to plan an anniversary celebration), *annus horribilis* (awful year, as used by Queen Elizabeth II), *bona fide* (genuine), *carpe diem* (seize the day), *caveat emptor* (buyer beware), CV (*curriculum vitae*, career summary), *mea culpa* (I am to blame), *pro bono* or *pro bono publico* (for the public good, as when a lawyer helps a charity without charge), *tempus fugit* (time flies).

Giving **plurals of foreign words** can be difficult: does one give them the plural they have in the original language, or an English plural? In one dictionary, *gâteau* becomes *gâteaux* but *château* can become *châteaux* or *châteaus* in the plural, although the latter is rejected by many. The plural of *femme fatale* is *femmes fatales*, showing that adjectives may need modifying to agree with plural nouns.

Adherents to the Queen's English aspire to correctness in all matters linguistic, even the use of foreign words in English. I predict that the use of accents will decline with time, so that words like *crêpe* and *crèche* will be more often used without those accents than with them. My advice is to carry on using the diacritical marks, at least for the present.

CHAPTER 23

New words, new meanings and changes in English

New words

The better you understand the use of **prefixes**, **suffixes** and **word origins** (pages 153–66), the better you can work out what new words mean, or even coin good new words yourself. New words are called **neologisms**, from *neo-*, new, plus *-logism*, from *logos*, word.

The **words or usages which arise or change most quickly** are those of **slang** and **technology**. With today's mass media, a new word or usage can spread rapidly round the English-speaking world. Children's slang and 'street slang' can change speedily. You need to keep up with these changes only if you deal with people who use them.

Changes in technology affect people to different extents. Computer users need to know the specialist uses of *mouse*, *cursor*, *surfing*, *browser*, *web*, *wizard*, *hacking*, *cookies* and *icon*, all of which have very different ordinary meanings.

Journalists love new usages, new words and new phrases, hoping to make their writing look fresh and contemporary.

An issue of the *Journal of the Royal Society of Medicine* had an article on 'A Wii problem'. It quoted amusing new medical words occasioned by Nintendo's 'Wii'. Injuries from over-enthusiastic use of such devices have been called *Nintendonitis*, *Playstation 2 Thumb*, the *Wii knee* and *Wiiitis*, which includes a rare triple '*i*'.

Before we had radio and TV, children grew up hearing English from their parents and local people, perhaps with local dialects and accents. Children are now exposed to many different forms of English from broadcasts, including much American English, with TV, videos and DVDs often used as 'babysitters'. Many broadcasts depart far from the Queen's English, with bad grammar and poor enunciation and pronunciation. There is no need to copy those faults.

The **core of English vocabulary** changes extremely slowly, which is why you can read with ease most works from two hundred years ago, or even further back, as in the King James Bible of 1611. The main source of new words today is technology. We still import words from abroad, and not just from America and Australia.

Some **words of foreign origin** have become so completely assimilated into English that their origins are not obvious, such as *skipper*, *landlubber*, *boom*, *sloop* and *nitwit*, all from Dutch. More recently adopted words sometimes stay largely associated with the country they came from, as with *samizdat*, *perestroika* and *glasnost* from Russia. See also pages 198–204 on foreign words and phrases.

Changes in parts of speech

An American claimed that *'There's no noun that can't be verbed'*.
Shakespeare 'verbed' several nouns in one sentence. In *King Lear*,
Act 1, Scene 1, Lear describes his daughter Cordelia as:

> *Unfriended, new-adopted to our hate.*
> *Dower'd with our curse, and stranger'd with our oath.*

Here, Shakespeare is using the past participle of a verb, *to stranger*,
a version of *to estrange*.

People now use parts of speech more interchangeably. In
particular, there are many cases of adjectives being used where
adverbs are needed. *The boys done good*, often used by football
managers, should be *The boys did well*. Such sloppy usage is not
the Queen's English. Nouns continue to be 'verbed', with varying
degrees of acceptability. *Access* used to be employed mainly as a
noun, but in libraries, information science and computing, it is
mainly used as a verb, *to access*. That is acceptable and avoids a
wordy circumlocution.

Google is a proper noun for an Internet search firm. We now
have a 'verbed' version, *to Google*, to look up on the Internet;
verbs with a capital letter are extremely rare. Words which began
as trademark-specific often become general: *to hoover* is used for
vacuum cleaning by any make of machine, not just a Hoover. The
Hollywood film industry promoted the use of the adjective *blonde*
as a noun.

Changes in meanings

Some words change their meaning radically over time, so one may
misinterpret terms in older books. For example, King Charles II

described the new St Paul's Cathedral as 'awful, artificial and amusing'; he meant, in our terms, 'awe-inspiring, artistic and amazing'. *Anorak*, in addition to meaning a hooded waterproof jacket (from the Inupiaq language), now also means a 'sad' person indulging in unfashionable pursuits.

Pejoration is where words acquire a derogatory meaning. In Jane Austen's *Pride and Prejudice*, Mr Collins uses *to demean oneself* to mean *to conduct oneself*, with no sense of debasement, but matching the sense of *demeanour*, behaviour. *Obsequious* used to mean *compliant* but now means *servile*, just as *officious* used to mean *dutiful* and *trustworthy*, but now means *pompously overbearing*. *Silly* once meant *blessed*, not *absurd*.

With **amelioration**, words lose a derogatory meaning. *Meticulous* used to mean *pernickety, over-zealous*, but now means *careful, conscientious*. *Sophisticated* has changed from meaning *corrupted, falsified*, to *elegant, cultured, polished*. An *enthusiast* is someone showing enthusiasm, no longer a *fanatic*.

Words can undergo a **narrowing** of meaning. *Corpse* was once a live or dead body, and a *deer* was any kind of animal, and used in that sense by Shakespeare. *Venison* was any sort of meat, and *fowl* any kind of bird. A *wife* once meant any woman, even if unmarried.

Other words have become **more general** in meaning. *Arrive* (note the resemblance to *river*) once meant coming to a river bank or shore, and *nausea* meant *seasickness*, not any kind of sickness.

Other changes in words

There is a strong tendency to use **shorter forms**, such as *photo* for *photograph*, *pub* for *public house*, *bike* for *bicycle*, *flu* for *influenza* and *bra* for *brassiere*. People often use shortened versions of their names. *Alex* could be female, *Alexandra*, or male, *Alexander*. Similarly, *Sam* could be female, *Samantha*, or male, *Samuel*.

Chairman is sometimes shortened to *Chair* to make it 'gender-neutral' but should never be *chair*. In the Queen's English Society we had two ladies who were happy to be called *Chairman*, taking the male term to embrace the female term; both were strongly against being called *Chair* or *chair*, an inanimate object.

Back in 1939, *The Daily Telegraph* used to put an apostrophe in front of plane, *'plane*, to show that *aero* had been omitted, and put hyphens where they are no longer used except by some pensioners: *to-morrow*, *to-day*. The same paper had *R.A.F.* for *Royal Air Force* in one article but *RAF* in another; it is best to be consistent.

Recent changes

24/7 has become common for '24 hours a day, seven days a week'. I do not like the use of *pressies* for *presents* or *invite* used as a noun instead of *invitation*, or *footie* for *football*. We have acronyms such as *WAGs* (wives and girlfriends – of sportsmen), *DINKY* (double income, no kids yet), and odd combinations such as *metrosexual* and *mockney*.

Language change is often influenced by **political movements**. I strongly believe in free speech and think that all lovers of English should oppose the emasculation of our language by political correctness.

When to adopt new words and usages

This is personal, so follow your inclinations. Consider the context and your readership or audience. Do you like to seem trendy or traditional? Could a new usage cause confusion, such as using *wicked* to mean *good*? The use of *gay* to mean *homosexual* is not a recent change but can still cause confusion and embarrassment.

There are good, useful new words, amusing new words, and bad new words and usages, especially ones leading to confusion of meanings. Be careful which you adopt.

Dictionaries and the acceptance of new words or meanings

When a **new edition of a dictionary** comes out, its publishers issue press releases with details of some of the new entries, especially odd ones which they hope that journalists will quote.

The new words in dictionaries are mainly from slang and technology, or adopted foreign words; they constitute an extremely small percentage of words in any new edition. People who write books about language change try to convince us that English changes rapidly, but most words stay much the same, which is why we can understand books from hundreds of years ago.

Dictionaries are treated as reputable, responsible authorities, to be used as referees in disputes about words. I believe that they have **a responsibility to the English language and its users**; they should try to maintain **clarity of meaning**. There are those who believe that dictionaries should be prescriptive, marking particular usages as wrong and others as correct or preferred. Most dictionary-makers prefer to consider dictionaries as **descriptive**, showing how language is used in practice, including errors.

If people make frequent errors in geography, history or maths, e.g., putting Auckland, not Wellington, as the capital of New Zealand, should that lead to the error being given as acceptable in geography books? Obviously not, but why should errors in English usage be regarded by dictionary-makers as acceptable if many people make them? I consider it wrong of dictionaries to blur different meanings, e.g., of *infer* and *imply* by listing *imply* as one meaning of *infer*.

If we lose distinctions between words, we get misunderstandings, loss of precision, and a poorer, less functional language. I am strongly in favour of dictionaries being prescriptive.

CHAPTER 24

Using English for humour and wit

The subtleties of English make it very suitable for **humour** and **wit**. While some jokes depend on embarrassing situations, the majority involve playing with language. Most great British humorists have had a deep knowledge of English and could therefore play wonderful tricks with it. Many jokes depend on puns, or taking idioms or figures of speech literally, as here:

> *On an icy day, how do you stop your mouth from freezing?*
> *You grit your teeth.*

The list of **types of joke** given here is not exhaustive. About one third of the jokes here are the author's; others are from books and the Internet.

Different kinds of humour appeal to different people, so consider your audience when making jokes.

Alliteration

Alliteration has word-beginnings sounding alike. This riddle has pleased children for many generations and is usually given in speech, not writing. It involves alliteration, rhyme, mispronunciation (misspelling if written) and elision:

Why couldn't the viper viper nose?

Because the adder adder 'ankerchief!

Doctor jokes

These often involve misunderstandings between doctors and patients, or mysterious ailments.

> Woman: *'Doctor, doctor. I've been pregnant for two years and don't know who the father is.'*
> Doctor: *'The milkman comes early, so it must be the postman. His deliveries are always late.'*
>
> Boy: *'Doctor, that cream you prescribed makes my arms smart.'*
> Doctor: *'Then try rubbing some on your head, sonny.'*

Dodgy definitions

These are fun to think up and spelling variations do not matter.

Alternatives: change the indigenous inhabitants.

Bumbling: flashy jewellery to decorate the posterior.

Coffee: the person coughed upon.

Deliverance: surgical removal of the liver.

Step-ladder: a device for climbing family trees where many parents with children have remarried.

Willy-nilly: impotent.

🐝 Errors

Unintentional **errors** can be very amusing. One of my UK students wrote about *insemination of these cows at the age of 3 with their fathers seamen*. Apart from the missing apostrophe, the mistake is the awful confusion of *seamen* with *semen*.

The following examples of errors are said to have been made by medical secretaries:

> *On the second day the knee was better and on the third day it had disappeared.*

> *Discharge status: Alive but without my permission.*

> *Examination of the patient's genitalia reveals that he is circus sized.*

✕ Limericks

Light verse gives enormous pleasure, although some stuffy poets deny that it is poetry. **Limericks** can pack so much humour and ingenuity into just five rhyming lines. Many classical poets wrote sexy limericks for private circulation. Here is a grammar-themed one of mine:

> **The wrong conjugation**
> *There was a young girl of Cadiz*
> *Whose character bubbled with fizz,*
> *But her terrible grammar*
> *Continued to damn'er,*
> *As she couldn't be cured of 'You is'.*

✕ Malapropisms

Malapropisms are confusions of vaguely similar words, named after Mrs Malaprop in Sheridan's 1775 play, *The Rivals*. His examples, put into her mouth, include:

> *an allegory on the banks of the Nile.* [alligator]

> *a nice derangement of epitaphs!* [arrangement of epigrams]

> *He is the very pine-apple of politeness!* [pinnacle]

'He is the very pine-apple of politeness!'

Misheard words

Jemima: *'On Valentine's Day I proposed to five different men
without avail.'*
Fiona: *'Try wearing a veil next time.'*

Paradoxes

Statements which seem contrary to common sense or self-
contradictory can be witty, intriguing and amusing. This is from
Oscar Wilde's play, *A Woman of No Importance*:

*The history of women is the history of the worst form of tyranny
the world has ever known. The tyranny of the weak over the
strong. It is the only tyranny that lasts.*

Puns

Puns play on the meanings of words, involving words sounding alike or words with the same spelling but different meanings: see pages 179–80. Although puns have been described as the lowest form of wit, they can be extremely funny when unexpected or outrageous.

> French frontier officer: *'Name, date and place of birth?'*
> German: *'General Fritz Schmidt, 14 May 1922, Berlin.'*
> Frenchman: *'Occupation?'*
> German: *'Nein, not zis time. Just a visit.'*

The pun is on two meanings of *occupation*.

Here is a classy pun on Santa Claus:

Santa's helpers are subordinate clauses.

Rhymes

In poems, plays, operettas or operas which use **rhyme**, the expectations created by the rhyming pattern can be exploited humorously by satisfying them with outrageously contrived rhymes, by using rare or made-up words, by breaking grammatical rules to achieve a rhyme, or by not satisfying those expectations.

In *The Mikado*, Gilbert rhymed *Lord High **Executioner*** with *very imperfect **ablutioner*** and *Of your pleasure a **diminutioner***. Neither of those words is in normal dictionaries, although the references to washing and reducing are clear.

Riddles

Riddles consist of short questions and answers, often involving puns.

> *What is a bachelor?*
> *A man who never Mrs a lady.*

Spelling/pronunciation mismatches

Many surnames and place names are pronounced differently from the way they are spelled, as in my limerick where *Leicester* sounds like *Lester* and *Norwich* like *Norridge*:

> *There was a young lady of Leicester*
> *Who said that that city Depreicester –*
> *When taken to Norwich*
> *And nurtured on Porwich*
> *Her spirits soon Reposseicester!*

Spoonerisms

Spoonerisms are named after the clergyman W. Spooner, who transposed the beginnings of words, as in *a well-boiled icicle*, instead of *a well-oiled bicycle*. Small differences in spelling do not matter.

> *What's the difference between a church bell and a thief? One peals from the steeple and the other steals from the people.*

CHAPTER 25

Giving talks: persuasion, passion and tone

This chapter deals with planned talks to groups, while pages 224–9 deal with spontaneous normal talk.

Setting the tone

Some of this advice applies to writing, not just to talks. Decide on what degree of formality will suit your audience. To set a **formal tone** for a speech, you might dress smartly, stand behind a lectern, and address your audience as 'Ladies and gentlemen'. To set an **informal tone**, you could wear casual clothes, and address the audience as 'Friends'. Which extreme or intermediate strategy you adopt depends on the occasion, the audience and personal preference.

Think carefully about the **purpose of the meeting**. Are you there to inform your audience, as in a lecture, or to amuse them? Are you chairing a meeting where important decisions need to be made, or are you asking people to vote for you?

It is good to **identify yourself with your audience**, as in 'Concerned fellow citizens of Norwich,' followed by lots of use of the pronoun 'we'. Establishing some kind of 'togetherness', or common ground and purpose, is very helpful for persuading people.

Delivering your speech, talk or lecture

- **How you deliver a speech** is important. It sets the tone and affects the audience's impressions. Try to appear relaxed and confident.
- A speech delivered apparently spontaneously, without notes, is more interesting and convincing than a speech read word-for-word. If you are afraid of missing important points or forgetting crucial figures, have the key items in large print on one sheet of paper.
- If you are delivering a **PowerPoint** lecture, or using a lot of overhead projector transparencies or photographic slides, keep it simple. If the audience has to read too many details, the effects can be dull.
- If you use **technology**, try it out in advance if possible. Make sure that you understand where all the controls are for the lights, projector, etc., if you have to operate them yourself.

- If the room is large and your voice is not powerful, **use a microphone** if one is available. Some of your audience may have poor hearing, especially if they are elderly.
- Consciously **project your voice** as if speaking to someone in the back row. Never talk down to your notes or towards a screen.
- Making **frequent eye contact** with the audience is most important. A speaker who does not look at the audience and who seems unaware of them is a poor speaker.
- **Cut out inessential details** that might mean something to you but not to your audience.
- **Keep your message as straightforward and as clear as you can,** using simple, approachable language and arguments. In a long speech, you should indicate at the start what it is about, why it is relevant to your audience, and the main points that you will try to cover. At the end, summarise the main points: don't just fade out.
- If appropriate, **ask for questions** at the end. Repeat each question for the audience, giving yourself time to think of an answer.
- If questioners ask for information which you do not have, then simply say you do not know, or that if they give you their details, you will find out and get back to them. **Address your answers to the whole audience.**

Passion or balance?

Provided that it is done well, a really **passionate speech** is far more persuasive than a balanced one. **If you are trying to convince your audience** of something then a totally biased presentation often works best, whatever the ethics of it might be.

If you are an impartial chairman, then summing up the case for or against some motion should be balanced, unemotional, not suppressing facts on either side of the case.

✂ General points

- For **maximum impact**, talks must be well organised, developed logically, and delivered clearly and smoothly. In an **oral presentation**, the listener has only one chance to grasp the material, unless the speaker repeats key points.
- Show your **awareness of your audience's interests**, concerns and knowledge. Where audiences vary greatly in that level, you can use phrases such as: '*I am sure that many of you know this already, but for those who don't* . . .'
- How you give the talk will depend a lot on its **purpose**. For example, if you are teaching a class for examination purposes, you must go at a suitable pace, and have enough light, for note-taking.
- You may wish to use **numbered points** to help organise your material and to help the audience follow how far you have got. If your talk seems like a series of flat statements, add variety by asking and answering questions.
- **Vary your pace, tone and delivery** to avoid monotony. Slow down to emphasise key points. If you start to run out of time, cut material rather than gabble, just summarising what you can no longer give in detail.

- If **time** is a problem, have a rehearsal on your own for timing purposes or persuade a friend or colleague to offer constructive criticism.
- It is hard for listeners to cope with large **numbers**. Could you easily follow 'six hundred and eighty-three thousand, nine hundred and eighty-four', and then seven other equally large numbers when spoken? Either give the numbers in a handout or put them on a screen, board or flipchart.
- **Your manner** should be warm and friendly, obviously caring about your audience, not aggressive or defensive. Use facial expressions and hand gestures to convey emotions.
- **Beware of distracting habits**. They include repeated fiddling with your hair, spectacles, clothing, a pointer or writing device. Ask a friend or colleague to let you know of any such habits. As with all aspects of speaking and writing, **constructive criticism** can be invaluable.

CHAPTER 26

Spoken English

This chapter is about **unscripted speech**, as in conversations or in broadcast interviews, unlike the chapter on giving prepared talks (pages 219–23).

Differences between spoken and written English

In speech, we often **omit words** that we would put in if writing.

Are you coming to the cinema with me tonight?

might in speech be shortened to:

Coming to the cinema tonight? or *Cinema tonight?*

When talking, we often put in **interjections** such as *um*, *er* or *ah*, while we pause to find the right word. We may start a sentence, then go back and recast it as we think of a better way to express the thought.

The former Director General of the BBC, Mark Thompson, is presumably normally a very fluent speaker. In December 2009 he was interviewed on the *Today* programme by author P. D. James, whose questions reduced him to near incoherence. Here are two sentences from his replies, as widely reported in the media and on the Internet:

Well, though, I think that, that if, like, like, you know, oth–,
other walks of life, I think most people will accept that if you
want to have the, um, the best people, um, er, working, er, for
the BBC, delivering the best programmes, the best services and
if you also accept that that means, particularly at a moment in
broadcasting history where people can move freely from the BBC
to other broadcasters and back, the BBC has to bear to some
extent in mind the external market, now, um, you know, if you
take, you know, someone who's going to be the controller of, of,
of BBC1, they're going to be spending about a billion pounds a
year, um, on television programmes for that channel.

We, we, the, it . . . the private broadcasters, as you know, are,
um, ITV, er, Channel 4 . . .

That illustrates the repetitions, the interjections, the losing track
of one's arguments and sentences, which can occur in speech,
especially under pressure.

Now contrast that example of **spontaneous spoken English**
with a **carefully planned speech**, broadcast to the nation by Sir
Winston Churchill on 4 June 1940. His wartime speeches avoided
many of these faults by being fully written out and revised several
times to increase their oratorical impact. He used deliberate
repetition to build up an effect in this stirring broadcast:

We shall go on to the end. We shall fight in France, we shall fight
on the seas and oceans, we shall fight with growing confidence
and growing strength in the air, we shall defend our island,
whatever the cost may be. We shall fight on the beaches, we shall
fight on the landing grounds, we shall fight in the fields and in the
streets, we shall fight in the hills; we shall never surrender.

We do many things unconsciously in speech. Please read these sentences aloud:

The banana and the apple tasted good.

The donkey and the ox were eating hay.

The energetic archer picked up the bow and arrow.

Did you notice a difference in your pronunciation of the word ***the*** before words starting with a consonant and those starting with a vowel? Try reading the sentences again. Although this is seldom taught in Britain, we tend to pronounce *the* as *ther*, with a short vowel sound, before a consonant, but as *thee*, with a long vowel sound, before words beginning with a vowel. In the last of those three sentences, did you run the last letter of *energetic* into the beginning of *archer*, or pronounce the last three words as *bo a narrow*?

In speech, we often **run words together**, leaving no audible gap between them, but the hearer's brain works out what was intended, usually correctly, based on sense, grammar and expectation. When a radio announcer mentions the composer *Jacques Ibert*, it often sounds like *Jacky Bert*.

We use *an*, not *a*, as the **indefinite article** before a word starting with a vowel sound: *an arrow*, *an old man*, but *a gun*, *a young man*. Note that we use *a*, not *an*, before an aspirated (breathy and sounded, not silent) *h*: *a hotel*, *a historic moment*. We would say *an hour*, as *hour* has a silent *h*.

For an interesting account of the differences between spoken and written English, see White's *Introducing the Grammar of Talk*, listed in the Bibliography.

Accents

People **change the way they speak** to give different impressions. In January 2010, the deputy leader of the Labour Party, Harriet Harman, described how she had quietly dropped her '1950s cut-glass accent' to fit in with her Labour Party colleagues, saying that in the 1970s, 'I sounded like Lady Diana.'

As George Bernard Shaw wrote in the preface to his play *Pygmalion*:

> *It is impossible for an Englishman to open his mouth, without making some other Englishman despise him.*

There is some truth in that. People tend to look down on those speaking less 'posh' or more 'posh' than themselves, or with different accents.

If you happen to – or choose to – pronounce *third* as *turd*, *South London* as *Sarf Lun'n*, and *butter* as *bu'er*, no one will arrest you for abusing the Queen's English. Those who speak the same way will admire you while those who do not will probably look down on you. The **glottal stop**, as in the middle of *bu'er* from omitting the consonants, is common in some areas and social strata.

There are books about **local accents**, such as Bristolian, where the old tradition was to add an 'l' to words ending in a vowel, as in *Queen Victorial; listen to the radiol*. The authors of such books collect many examples to make a whole book but very few locals employ even half of them. How many people talk pure Cockney in London today?

Clarity of speech

What is important is **clarity of diction**, not blurring your words or talking to your hand rather than to the person you are addressing. You do not have to 'talk posh' to speak clearly. Be aware that local usages may not be understood by people elsewhere. It is polite to look at the people to whom you are speaking. You can see from their reactions whether they are understanding you. Slow down if they seem to be struggling.

To hear **exemplary clear speech,** listen to the morning newsreaders on BBC Radio 3. At present, they nearly all speak excellent unaccented English, with what has been called 'received pronunciation', 'BBC English' or 'Oxford English'. Many radio and television programmes have awful examples of poor speech.

CHAPTER 27

Further self-tests

Identify the errors and decide how to correct them. Most examples are real; a few are made up. In the biological items, the errors of English should be clear without specialist biological knowledge.

1. *The compound breaks down with time and looses its inhibitory effect.*
2. *We filled new barrels completely with cold water (about 220C) for 24 hours to let the staves re-hydrate.*
3. *Storing barrels on purpose made racks or even 3 on a pallet is very handy as you can move them about with a palate truck or fork lift.*
4. *The warp and weft of curriculum design is meshed through a competency based, holistic view of student learning.*
5. *'I couldn't believe it when they sent me an email telling me that my Dad's Army board game could insight violence and hatred.'*
6. *Neither sport has featured at the Albert Hall for around a decade, and the management failed to include them when it reapplied for a license following a change in the law in 2005.*
7. *This is particularly evident in Praa Sands, East of Penzance, where the geology and erosion has earned the area Site of Special Scientific Interest status.*
8. *Although there are many complicating factors (such as the affects of new ICT), teachers know that more than a decade of teaching*

to the test and prescriptive literacy and numeracy strategies have left students overschooled and undereducated.

9. Principals of treatment of exacerbations associated with emerging resistant bacteria. [A heading]

10. With just a roll of sticky white labels (£1.99 for 500 from most stationary stores) you can reuse every envelope which comes through your door.

11. The numbers of errors in each generation was more, not less, than what went before.

12. He travelled extensively and visited the courts in Europe were he was offered a wealth of opportunities.

13. His father, a lawyer, died when he was ten years old.

14. One bacteria and two fungus were plated on three mediums as seperate colonies.

15. The price that a breeder might get for his cow would depend on how many prizes he had got and not on his siring ability.

16. This book is based on lectures and clinical demonstrations of venereal diseases which the author has been giving to undergraduates for many years.

17. His first law states that he thought characters where past on from generation to generation by particulate factors.

18. The male fruit fly possesses sex combs on its front legs. These are not present in the female.

19. Short plants will only be produced in the absence of tall genes.

20. The fact of having sexes infers the process of sexual reproduction.

21. To finish we had figs roasted with port, nuts, coffee, and petit fours.

22. It was a similar winter, some years ago, that convinced Sid he needed a live in farm hand.

23. Continental breakfast was served in the Orangery, again peering down on a mist shrouded Thames.

24. *Today Sparrow's Vancouver based company, Saltworks Technologies Inc. is on the final development of a saltwater powered battery.*

25. *I was literally dead with fatigue.*

26. *People, who live in glass houses, shouldn't throw stones.*

27. *Personally, I think that English scholars often disagree with each other.*

28. *He was confidant that his affectations for her would soon illicit her love.*

29. *In the currant circumstances, it is essential to insure that you meet all our criterions.*

30. *It was pelting down with rain, the roads were soon running like rivers in spait.*

ANSWERS TO FURTHER SELF-TESTS

1. *Loses* was intended.

2. 220C should be 22°C.

3. *Purpose-made* racks (compound adjective); *three*; *pallet* truck.

4. Compound subject, so *is* should be *are*. *Competency-based.*

5. *Incite*, not *insight*.

6. *Licence* (noun).

7. *East* should be *east*. Geology and erosion *have*.

8. *Effects*, not affects.

9. *Principles*. The lack of a finite verb does not matter in a heading.

10. *Stationery*.

11. *Were* more. Not *fewer*.

12. *Where*, not *were*.

13. Pronoun ambiguity. Who died aged ten?

14. *Bacterium, fungi, media, separate.*

15. Muddled! As cows are female, *he* presumably refers to the farmer. The student probably meant *bull* rather than *cow*.

16. Ambiguity. Did the lecturer give his students venereal diseases? Recast as two sentences.

17. Laws do not state that someone thinks. *Were*, not *where*. *Passed* on, not *past*.

18. *These* should relate to sex combs, not front legs. *Its* perhaps should be *his*.

19. Genes for tallness, not tall genes.

20. *Implies*, not *infers*.

21. Were the figs roasted with all those following items? Extra punctuation or words are needed. The plural of *petit four* is *petits fours*: the adjective needs modifying to agree with the plural noun.

22. *Live-in*. Farm hand could be put as one word.

23. Peering, etc.; this is a hanging phrase, with no subject. *Mist-shrouded*.

24. *Vancouver-based*. Comma needed after Inc. as one of a pair. *Saltwater-powered*.

25. Misuse of *literally*.

26. Both commas are wrong; with those commas, the part between them is a non-restrictive clause but should be restrictive as not all people live in glass houses.

27. *Personally* is redundant. Ambiguity: scholars of English or scholars from England?

28. *Confident*. Presumably *affections*. *Elicit*.

29. *Current*. *Ensure* is more likely than *insure* in this context. *Criteria*.

30. *Spate*. Splice comma; a semicolon or colon is needed to join these two separate sentences.

Glossary

This glossary summarises the main grammatical terms used in this book, but not the punctuation marks, which are described on pages 96–121.

Abstract noun A noun describing things which cannot be touched, seen, heard, smelled or tasted, e.g., *love*.

Active voice A verb's active voice shows that the subject is performing the action, not having it done to the subject, e.g., *He strikes*.

Adjective A word that modifies and describes a noun or pronoun, e.g., *ruddy*.

Adverb A word that modifies a verb, adjective or adverb, e.g., *quickly*.

Antonym A word with the opposite meaning to another, e.g., *sweet* is an antonym of *sour*.

Article The words *a* and *an* are **indefinite articles**, referring to a general item, such as *an apple*, while the **definite article**, *the*, refers to a particular item such as *the apple*.

Auxiliary verb A verb which combines with the main verb to show differences in person, tense or voice, e.g., *I **will** go*.

Case The state of a noun or pronoun reflecting its function as a subject, e.g., *he*; an object, *him*; or a possessor, *his*.

Clause A group of related words containing a subject and its finite verb.

Cliché An overused phrase or comparison, e.g., *as dry as dust*.

Collective noun A noun encompassing a group of people or things, e.g., *committee, team*.

Common noun A noun which does not need an initial capital letter, describing an object, place or person, e.g., *wall, town, woman*.

Complex sentence A sentence made up of a main clause and one or more subordinate clauses.

Compound adjective A combination of two or more words making an adjective and usually needing a hyphen unless one word is an adverb, e.g., *a **high-risk** strategy*.

Compound sentence A sentence made by joining two or more simple sentences by a conjunction, comma, semicolon or colon.

Conjunction A word joining words, phrases, clauses or sentences, e.g., *and, if*.

Consonant Any letter of the alphabet except the vowels *a, e, i, o* and *u*, e.g., *c*.

Continuous tense A tense where the action is continuing, e.g., *She is cycling*.

Demonstrative adjective An adjective used to point out something, e.g., *this, that*.

Dependent clause The same as a subordinate clause: a group of words with a subject and its verb, but subordinate to the main clause, e.g., *The dog hated him **because he never gave it any exercise***.

Determiners are words going before nouns or noun phrases and which limit their meaning. They include numbers, articles and demonstrative and possessive adjectives, e.g., *three*, *the*, *this*, *my*.

Direct object A noun or pronoun receiving the action of a transitive verb, e.g., *The dog bit **him***.

Etymology The origins of words and the study of those origins.

Finite verb A verb limited by person, tense, voice and mood, e.g., *She **wept***.

Gerund A verb's participle acting as a noun, which can take adjectives and act as subject or object, e.g., *The cruel **killing** was abhorrent*.

Hanging phrase or dangling participle A phrase which is unrelated to the rest of the sentence, usually containing a participle, not a finite verb, e.g., ***Driving very fast***, *the dog stood no chance*. It was not the dog who was driving.

Homograph Different words are homographs if spelled the same way, e.g., *sow* (plant seeds), *sow* (female pig).

Homophone Words are homophones if pronounced the same way, e.g., *rays, raze, raise*.

Indirect object A noun or pronoun to whom, to what or for what the action of a transitive verb is performed, although it is not the direct object, e.g., *He gave **her** a kiss*. Here *kiss* is the direct object, what was given, to *her*, the indirect object.

Infinitive The basic form of a verb, not limited by person, tense, mood or voice, and usually given together with the participle *to*, e.g., *to see*.

Interjection A word or words used as an exclamation, e.g., *Ah!*

Intransitive verb A verb which does not have a direct object, e.g., *They **sleep***.

Main clause A group of words containing a subject and its finite verb, and which can make sense on its own, unlike a subordinate clause, e.g., **The dog hated him** *because he never gave it any exercise*.

Metaphor The application of a description which is imaginative, not literal, without an introductory term such as *like*, e.g., *You are **a horny old goat***.

Modifier A dependent word or phrase modifying the meaning of a main word or expression. Modifiers include adjectives, adverbs or nouns, e.g., *a **yellow** dress*.

Mood The mood of a verb can be *indicative* (ordinary statements), *imperative* (when orders are given) or *subjunctive* (suppositions, wishes, hopes, imagination, doubts and proposals).

Noun A word used to name a person, place or thing, e.g., *Alice, village, rhubarb*.

Object The object receives the action of a transitive verb, e.g., *He berated **his audience***.

Paragraph A delimited section of writing consisting of one or more sentences, usually but not necessarily covering one topic.

Participle A part of a verb which can also function as an adjective but not as a complete verb. The present participle often ends in *-ing*, e.g., *lying*, as in *you **lying** hound*. The past participle follows *has* or *have* in the past tense, and often ends in *-ed*, e.g., *he has **jumped***.

Passive voice In the passive voice, the subject has the action done to it, e.g., *The speaker was heckled*.

Perfect tense A tense where the action has been completed, usually formed with the auxiliary verb *to have*, e.g., *He **had shot** the fox*.

Phrasal verb A multiword combination of a verb with one or more adverbs or prepositions, or sometimes both, making a complete unit, e.g., *They **passed out** from the effects of the toxic gas.*

Phrase A group of related words but not making a complete clause or sentence, perhaps from lacking a finite verb, e.g., *the old, weary man.*

Possessive adjective An adjective showing possession, e.g., ***your** intellect.*

Prefix A set of one or more letters added at the beginning of a word and affecting its meaning, e.g., *un-* in ***un**necessary.*

Preposition A word showing the relation (often spatial) between nouns or pronouns in a sentence, e.g., *The cat sat **on** the chair.*

Pronoun A word standing for a noun, e.g., *John ran; **he** was late.*

Proper noun A noun referring to a particular person, place or thing, not to one of a general class; such nouns start with a capital letter, e.g., *Mary, Aberdeen,* the *Reform Club.*

Received pronunciation Standard English pronunciation with no regional or ethnic accent; formerly called *BBC English* or *Oxford English.*

Relative clause A clause introduced by a relative pronoun (e.g., *who, which* or *that*), or by a relative adverb (e.g., *where, why, when*), e.g., *The village **which I had loved as a child** was now spoiled.*

Relative pronoun A pronoun which links a subordinate clause to the main clause, e.g., *who, which, what, whoever,* as in *The man, **who** was a complete idiot, ran suddenly into the traffic.*

Restrictive phrase or clause A phrase or clause which restricts the meaning of the sentence part to which it applies; it is not just a comment, but is defining, e.g., *Runners **who are in poor condition** endanger their health.* This means that only runners who are in poor condition endanger their health. To enclose the restrictive clause, *who are in poor condition*, in commas would make it non-restrictive, just commenting, and would change the meaning.

Sentence A group of words, rarely one word, which makes sense on its own.

Simile A comparison made using introductory words such as *like* or *as*, e.g., *Melanie was like a delicate flower*.

Subject The noun or pronoun which a sentence is about and to which the main verb applies, e.g., ***Jennifer*** *is a brilliant manager*.

Subordinate clause A clause which does not make sense on its own and depends on the main clause, e g , *The policeman*, ***who was a jovial old character***, *retired last week*.

Suffix A letter or group of letters added to the end of a word to change its meaning or grammatical role, e.g., *normal* [adjective], *normally* [adverb].

Synonym Synonyms are words with the same or almost identical meanings, e.g., *start*, *beginning*.

Tense The aspect of a verb which conveys the time of action, e.g., *past*, *present* or *future*.

Transitive verb One where action is conveyed by the subject to the object, e.g., *He* ***smashed*** *the vase*.

Verb A word or group of words expressing a subject's action or state of being, e.g., *She* ***cries***. *She* ***is*** *sad*.

Voice The character of a verb in being active or passive, depending whether the subject does the action or receives it. Active voice: *He hit the ball*. Passive voice: *He was hit by the ball*.

Vowel Any of the letters *a*, *e*, *i*, *o* and *u*; *y* sometimes behaves like a vowel although it is a consonant.

Bibliography

Later editions than those listed may be available.

Ayto, J. and I. Crofton, *Brewer's Dictionary of Modern Phrase & Fable*, 2nd edition. Weidenfeld & Nicolson, 2006.

Brewer's Dictionary of Phrase & Fable, 18th edition, edited by C. Rockwood. Chambers Harrap, 2005.

Bruton-Simmonds, I., *Mend Your English, or What We Should Have Been Taught At Primary School*, revised international edition, revised by B. C. Lamb. Ivy Publications, 2010.

Chalker, C. and E. Weiner, *The Oxford Dictionary of English Grammar*. Oxford University Press, 1994.

The Chambers Dictionary, 11th edition. Chambers Harrap, 2009.

Chambers Dictionary of Etymology, edited by R. K. Barnhart. Chambers Harrap, 2008.

Collins English Dictionary, 9th edition. HarperCollins, 2007.

Concise Oxford Dictionary, 11th revised edition, edited by C. Soanes and A. Stevenson. Oxford University Press, 2004.

Corbeil, J.-C. and M. Manser, *Visual Dictionary*. Facts on File Publications, 1988. This collection of labelled illustrations often enables one to find a word, e.g., for a part of a window, of a Greek temple or of a horse.

Dummett, M., *Grammar and Style for Examination Candidates and Others*. Gerald Duckworth & Co. Ltd., 1993.

Flavell, L. and R. Flavell, *The Chronology of Words and Phrases: A Thousand Years in the History of English*. Silverdale Books, 1999.

Gee, R. and C. Watson, *The Usborne Book of Better English: Grammar, Spelling and Punctuation*. Usborne Publishing Ltd., 1990. This is excellent for children and adults.

Heffer, S. *Strictly English: the Correct Way to Write... and Why it Matters*. Windmill Books, 2011.

Heller, L. and others, *The Private Lives of English Words*. Routledge & Kegan Paul, 1984.

Lamb, B. C., *The Queen's English Society's Practical Guide to Punctuation*. The Queen's English Society, 2008

Lamb, B., I. Harrison and R. Harrison, *English for Technology: Steps to Subject-specific Language Teaching*. City Technology Colleges Trust, 1995.

The New Fowler's Modern English, 3rd edition, edited by R. W. Burchfield. Clarendon Press, Oxford, 1996.

Newman, S. and D. Stark, *Collins Million Word Crossword Dictionary*. HarperCollins, 2005.

The Origins of Words & Phrases. The Reader's Digest Association Ltd., 2008.

Oxford English Dictionary, 2nd edition. Oxford University Press, 1989. A colossal and authoritative work, often available electronically through public libraries. Very good on word history.

Partridge, E., *Usage and Abusage: A Guide to Good English*, 3rd edition, revised by J. Whitcut. Penguin Books, 1999.

Pechenik, J. A. and B. C. Lamb, *How to Write about Biology*. HarperCollins College Division, 1994.

Peck, J. and M. Coyle, *The Student's Guide to Writing: Spelling,*

Punctuation and Grammar, 2nd edition. Palgrave Macmillan, 2005.

Rodale, J. I., *The Synonym Finder*, revised by L. Urdang and N. LaRoche. Rodale Press, 1979.

Roget's Thesaurus of English Words & Phrases, new edition by G. Davidson. Penguin, 2004.

Stedman's Concise Medical and Allied Health Dictionary, illustrated 3rd edition, edited by J. H. Dirckx. Williams & Williams, 1997.

Strunk, W. and E. B. White, *The Elements of Style*, 4th edition. Longman, 2000.

Truss, L., *Eats, Shoots & Leaves: The Zero Tolerance Approach to Punctuation*. Fourth Estate, 2009.

White, J., *Introducing the Grammar of Talk*. QCA, National Curriculum English, Key Stages 3–4, 2004.

Writers' & Artists' Yearbook 2010. A & C Black. (updated annually)

The Writer's Handbook 2010, edited by B. Turner. Macmillan. (updated annually)

The Queen's English Society

Aims

The Queen's English Society aims to promote good English and to discourage bad English. It encourages people to know more about English, to enjoy it more and to use it more effectively.

Its objects are to promote the knowledge, understanding and appreciation of written and spoken English, especially British English. We wish to encourage the education of the public in the correct, elegant and efficient usage of the language, discouraging anything detrimental to clarity of meaning or beauty of sound. It is our privilege to have such an expressive language with a huge vocabulary, so that very delicate shades of meaning are possible. It can be rich and elegant or blunt and plain, according to need.

We aim to draw the attention of the public and the media to the appallingly low standards of English of many school leavers and graduates, and to some poor standards of English writing and speech in the media and commerce. We have done this by means of surveys which have received extensive publicity in the press, on radio and TV. Some of our survey results have been quoted by Secretaries of State for Education and in the House of Lords.

Through contributions to the work of the Qualifications and Curriculum Authority and our responses to government

243

enquiries, we have encouraged the specification of the National Curriculum English Order to include more on grammar, spelling and punctuation. Even though that Order looks fairly satisfactory on paper, it is not being implemented well enough in the schools, judging by the English of so many school leavers, even if they have paper qualifications in English. We wish to work with teachers to improve standards.

We hold occasional national conferences on relevant topics. We have links with other national societies which share some of our aims, including the Campaign for Real Education, the Prayer Book Society and the Plain Language Commission. We are also a registered charity, No. 27290.

Background

The Queen's English Society is open to everyone, with no qualifications or expertise required, just an interest in our language and sympathy with our aims. Our members have very diverse backgrounds in education, geographical origin, race, culture, occupation, politics, age and accent. We are particularly strong in experts on the teaching of reading. The late Dr Joyce Morris, OBE, was one of our patrons.

You do not have to speak in 'received pronunciation' to belong. We have members in other countries and on other continents, all caring about the English language.

Our members include working or retired teachers, university lecturers, scientists, medical doctors, people in the theatre, arts and business, broadcasters, journalists, librarians, groundsmen, secretaries, accountants, computer specialists, linguists and translators, poets, writers, housewives, students, hotel workers, transport workers, and so on. Some are happy just to receive our magazine *Quest* and the newsletter, which are both published three times a year. Others attend meetings nationally in London for the summer luncheon and the Annual General Meeting, or branch meetings in London and Sussex.

History and achievements

The Queen's English Society was founded in 1972 by Joe Clifton, an Oxford graduate and schoolteacher. A letter he sent to his local newspaper (the *West Sussex Gazette*) deploring the current decline in standards of English resulted in so many sympathetic letters that he was encouraged to form a group to try to do something about the problem.

Meetings of the newly formed Society were held in Arundel. Members wrote to newspapers and others responsible for producing printed material, pointing out errors and examples of the misuse of English. Concern was also expressed about mispronunciation by broadcasters, and instances of their bad spoken English were highlighted in the hope that they would not be repeated.

The Society has always been very concerned about the education of children. Standards depend on how well those who have influence were taught, and on whether they care about English. When, in 1988, it became evident that most schools were no longer teaching English well enough, the Society delivered a petition to Kenneth Baker, the Secretary of State for Education and Science, urging him 'to introduce the compulsory study of formal grammar, including parsing and sentence analysis, into the school curriculum'. This attracted widespread support and resulted in many new (and distinguished) members.

We have produced four major surveys which have achieved national and international publicity. The first (published in 1992) investigated UK undergraduates' standards of English and the second (1994) the communication skills of young entrants to industry and commerce. On the day of publication, the latter's author gave seventeen radio and TV interviews. A third survey was published in 1997, on the opinions and practices of teachers of English to pupils aged 11–18. Those three surveys were published as books and have been referred to by writers of books about standards in English.

Our last main survey was published in our journal, *Quest*, in November 2009. It showed that home undergraduates at Imperial College London made three times more errors in English than did the overseas students. Compared with the students from China, Singapore and Indonesia, the home students were worse at grammar and spelling, and much worse with word confusions and the use of apostrophes and other punctuation marks. These were results from English in use for degree purposes, not some one-off test in which the home students might have played up.

Again, there was worldwide publicity. The study showed that even very bright home students, at one of the three top universities in the UK, leave school with inadequate English. Some of the errors seem incredible, from non-dyslexic students. Standards are much lower again for the average leaver from a 'bog-standard' comprehensive school.

One of our activities is to respond to media requests for interviews when some aspect of English is in the news. The topics have ranged widely, from education to poetry, from apostrophes and spelling to texting.

As well as our survey books, we have published our conference proceedings, a practical guide to punctuation, and a book of selected articles from *Quest*. Details are given below.

☙ Principal publications

Quest, the journal of the Queen's English Society, now published three times a year, alternating with the newsletter.

B. C. Lamb, *A National Survey of UK Undergraduates' Standards of English*, 1992.

B. C. Lamb, *A National Survey of Communication Skills of Young Entrants to Industry and Commerce*, 1994.

B. C. Lamb, *The Opinions and Practices of Teachers of English: A National Survey of Teachers of English to 11–18-year-olds, by the Queen's English Society*, 1997.

B. C. Lamb, *The Queen's English Society's Practical Guide to Punctuation*, 2008.

B. C. Lamb, 'British undergraduates make three times as many errors in English as do those from overseas.' *Quest* 103, pp. 12–18, 2009.

Shakin' the Ketchup Bot'le: An English Language Sauce Book, 2009. [Collected items from *Quest*.]

The Queen's English Society Silver Jubilee Conference: Controversial Issues in English, edited by J. M. Morris, 1997.

☙ Website

www.queens-english-society.org

The website gives general information about the Queen's English Society, including its aims and how to join, and contains a number of helpful articles giving advice on various aspects of English. The more members we have, the greater our chance of influencing standards of English through our campaigns and personal contacts.

There is no English Academy to match the Académie française for French, or the Academia Real de la Lengua Española for Spanish, to regulate the use of the language and act as guardian of the literary heritage. It is arguable whether an English Academy would be useful today, and the QES sees its role as giving guidance rather than being an authority. This book and the website are our main channels for guidance.

The QES website is gradually being enlarged with material designed to enhance the knowledge, understanding and use of proper English. There are items on points of grammar, punctuation and spelling, concentrating on those which often cause difficulty and errors. Planned sections include self-tests with answers, similar to those in this book, as testing one's knowledge in various areas of English can be very helpful in showing where improvements are needed.

Index

Principal locations for entries are denoted in **bold**